THE UNOFFICIAL GUIDE TO

Hockey's Most Unusual Records

The Unofficial Guide to
HOCKEY'S
MOST
Don Weekes &
Kerry Banks
UNUSUAL
RECORDS

GREYSTONE BOOKS

Douglas & McIntyre Publishing Group

Vancouver/Toronto/Berkeley

For everyone who wants more out of hockey.

Copyright © 2002 by Don Weekes and Kerry Banks
First U.S. edition in 2004
04 05 06   5 4 3

Greystone Books
A division of Douglas & McIntyre Ltd.
2323 Quebec Street, Suite 201
Vancouver, British Columbia
Canada V5T 4S7
www.greystonebooks.com

National Library of Canada Cataloguing in Publication Data
Weekes, Don
    The unofficial guide to hockey's most unusual records

    ISBN: 1-55054-942-1

    1. National Hockey League—Miscellanea. 2. Hockey—Miscellanea.
I. Banks, Kerry, 1952– II. Title.
GV847.W442 2002   796.962'64   C2002-910698-2

Library of Congress information is available upon request.

Editing by Christine Kondo
Cover and interior design by Peter Cocking
Cover photographs by Bruce Bennett/Bruce Bennett Studios
Typeset by Tanya Lloyd Kyi
Printed and bound in Canada by Friesens
Printed on acid-free paper
Distributed in the U.S. by Publishers Group West

We gratefully acknowledge the financial support of the Canada Council for the
Arts, the British Columbia Ministry of Tourism, Small Business and Culture, and
the Government of Canada through the Book Publishing Industry Development
Program (BPIDP) for our publishing activities.

DON WEEKES *is an award-winning television producer-director at* CTV *in Montreal.
He has written 19 hockey trivia books.*
KERRY BANKS *is an award-winning magazine journalist and sports columnist with
Vancouver's* Georgia Straight. *He is the author of 10 books including* Pavel Bure: The
Riddle of the Russian Rocket *and four previous titles in the* Hockey Heroes *series.*

Contents

Introduction

The idea behind this book was simple, and more than a little insane. We wanted to compile all the hockey records that you can't find anywhere else, and publish them in one handy, pocket-sized reference source. Our intent was to go beyond the standard statistical fare into the twilight world of hockey arcana—presenting records not only of rare achievement but also of abject failure; weird and wacky stuff; records that answered the questions we often asked but for which we could never find an answer.

In other words, we wanted to produce exactly the type of record book we would like to own.

Of course, there is a good reason why this sort of book has never been done before. It is fiendishly difficult to compile records that don't already exist in some computerized data bank. Assembling this material from a myriad of sources—the Internet, books, magazines, game summaries, library archives, plus a whack of original research—was exhausting, not to mention hard on the eyes. Now that it's finally done, we are both on the waiting list for cornea transplants.

Welcome to the *Unofficial Guide to Hockey's Most Unusual Records*. It's the sort of book that stands up and bangs the rink glass and screams, "Wayne Gretzky doesn't own 61 NHL records, he owns 62." His 62nd may be his most revered: most records set by a player in an NHL career.

So, here they are: the record for the largest bribe offered by a player, the fastest slap shot, the fewest shots on net by a 50-goal scorer, the largest octopus ever tossed onto the ice, the most fighting majors in a career, the fewest games missed in a 20-year span, the most future Hall of Famers on a Cup winner, the most stitches amassed by a maskless goalie, and much, much more.

Hey, don't be afraid to slam the rink glass. The closer you are to the action, the better it gets.

DON WEEKES & KERRY BANKS
June 2002

CHAPTER 1

Game on

The NHL's toughest records to break? Try Wayne Gretzky's 215-point season, Phil Esposito's 550 regular-season shot count, Darryl Sittler's 10-point game, Glenn Hall's 502-game ironman streak or Terry Sawchuk's 103 career shutouts. How about Philly's 35-game unbeaten streak, Montreal's famous five-in-a-row Cup run or Eddie Shack's unlikely selection as All-Star MVP in 1962. Records are meant to be broken. Here are some that break all the rules.

Most famous hockey nickname

The Great One: Wayne Gretzky, 1979–80 to 1998–99
The Rocket: Maurice Richard, 1942–43 to 1959–60

Most players given the same nickname

17: Red
Imaginative it is not, popular it is. At least 17 flame-haired NHLers have been nicknamed Red, including Red Kelly, Red Berenson, Red Horner and Red Sullivan.

Most nicknames belonging to one player
5: Howie Morenz, 1923–24 to 1936–37

Morenz, the NHL's first superstar, earned five well-known monikers: The Canadian Comet, The Hurtling Habitant, The Mitchell Meteor, The Stratford Streak and The Babe Ruth of Hockey.

Most disparaging nicknames on one scoring line

3: The Production Line, Detroit, 1950s
The NHL's most dangerous offensive force during the early 1950s was Detroit's Production Line. Not only did Gordie Howe, Sid Abel and Ted Lindsay have a lethal touch around the net, they also had three unflattering nicknames: Blinky, Boot Nose and Scarface. Keeping the tradition intact, when the Red Wings traded Abel to Chicago in 1952, he was replaced at centre on the line by Alex Delvecchio, who was known as Fats.

Length of the shortest player surname

3 letters
Several players, including Patrick Roy, Ron Low, Eddie Mio and Peter Ing.

Length of the longest player surname

14 letters

John Brackenborough's name had seven more letters than his total number of NHL games. Born in Parry Sound, Ontario, the centre played briefly for Boston in 1925–26.

Height of the tallest player

Six foot nine: Zdeno Chara, 1997–98 to 2001–02

The Czech-born Goliath is eight inches taller than the average NHLer at six foot one. He tips the scales at 255 lbs.

Height of the tallest goaltender

Six foot five: Steve Valiquette, 1999–2000

Valiquette, at six foot five and 206 pounds, may be the biggest netminder of all time, but his career has been extremely short: six games with the NY Islanders in 1999–2000.

Height of the shortest player

ALL-TIME RECORD

Five foot three: Roy "Shrimp" Worters, 1925–26 to 1936–37

Worters always played bigger than his size (he stood barely a foot above the crossbar), winning the Hart Trophy as MVP in 1928–29 and the Vezina Trophy as top netminder in 1930–31. Soaking wet he weighed 135 pounds.

MODERN-DAY RECORD

Five foot five: Bobby Lalonde, 1971–72 to 1981–82

Five foot five: Darren Pang, 1984–85 to 1988–89

Despite his diminutive stature, the 155-pound Lalonde played 641 NHL games, recording 334 points with Vancouver, Atlanta, Boston and Calgary. Pang, a goalie, played 81 games with Chicago.

Height of the shortest goaltender

Five foot three: Roy "Shrimp" Worters, 1925–26 to 1936–37

Five foot four: Connie Dion, 1943–44 to 1944–45

Fastest skater
Mike Gartner, 1979–80 to 1997–98

Gartner was clocked in the all-time fastest time of 13.386 seconds at the NHL All-Star game's fastest-skater competition.

Fastest registered NHL slapshot

ALL-TIME RECORD

118.3 MPH: Bobby Hull, 1957–58 to 1979–80

The accuracy of Hull's amazing record is questionable. Timing devices in his era were not as exact as they are today.

CURRENT RECORD

105.2 MPH: Al Iafrate, 1993

Shooting left, using a Koho Revolution 2240 stick, Iafrate's howitzer was registered at the Hardest Shot competition at the 1993 NHL All-Star game. Who has the hardest boomer in game situations? A few NHL goalies believe that distinction belongs to others such as Brett Hull and Al MacInnis, which supports the theory that some players slyly hold back their best stuff at All-Star competitions.

Largest hockey stick

207 feet: Duncan Community Centre, British Columbia

107 feet: USA Hockey Hall of Fame, Eveleth, Minnesota

Both sites claim this record. The Americans insist their stick is real because it's made from one piece of solid aspen, while the Canadian stick is constructed from several pieces of solid wood.

Most hockey sticks used, one season

700: Wayne Gretzky, Edmonton, 1984–85

As Bruce Dowbiggin notes in his book *The Stick: A History, A Celebration, an Elegy,* "Gretzky, in his prime, went through six sticks a game, some 700 a year, though he rarely broke one. In part it was superstition, in part the voracious demand for souvenirs."

Most hockey sticks used by a player in his final game

40: Wayne Gretzky, NY Rangers, April 18, 1999

Gretzky used as many as 40 sticks in his final NHL game, keeping them to donate to charitable functions or to pass on to friends and teammates.

Most stitches, career

978: Eddie Shore, 1926–27 to 1939–40

The rugged Boston defenseman was a poster boy for punishment. In addition to his 900-plus stitches, Shore also suffered fractures to his hip, back and collarbone, had his nose broken 14 times and his jaw cracked five times. Surprisingly, for someone cut so often, Shore was virtually scar-free. He credited this to his practice of diligently massaging the places on his face where he had been stitched up.

Most stitches by a goaltender, career

400: Terry Sawchuk, 1949–50 to 1969–70

Sawchuk received more than 400 stitches in his face, including three in his right eyeball, before donning a mask in 1962.

Most stitches, one game

300: Borje Salming, Toronto, November 1982

This nasty injury occurred when Detroit's Gord Gallant stepped on Salming's face during a goalmouth scramble. The skate blade sliced the skin above the Leafs defenseman's right eye, and cut deeply into his nose and down the side of his face. Sealing the wound required 300 stiches and three hours of surgery. Salming was sent home from the hospital with his face a patchwork quilt of sutures that crisscrossed his forehead, ran past one eye, across his nose, back under the eye, down his cheek and ended at the corner of his mouth. Salming donned a visor after his injury.

Most knee surgeries, career
11: Gord Kluzak, Boston, 1982–83 to 1990–91
The big defenseman out of Climax, Saksatchewan, was the first overall pick in the 1982 entry draft. But the bright future that the Bruins envisioned for Kluzak never materialized. The blueliner spent almost as much time in the operating room as he did on the ice. After playing two full seasons, he underwent 11 knee surgeries in the last seven years of his career.

Most fans with missing teeth at a pro hockey game, by an official count
269: IHL Kansas City Blades, April 17, 1999
As part of a promotion, 269 fans with missing teeth were admitted free on Toothless Night.

Most games attended by fans, one night
3: Joel Bierenbaum, Julian Kaplan, Steven Lefland and Mike Eisenberg, March 3, 1983
The first time the New Jersey Devils, NY Rangers and NY Islanders all played at home on the same night, four hockey fans made history by attending one period of the

three games in three different rinks. And they never broke
the speed limit, catching the first period in New Jersey,
the second at Madison Square Garden and the third at
Nassau Coliseum.

Most NHL arenas played in by a player, career

50 or more
Several players, including Gary Suter, Ron Sutter and Vincent
Damphousse, who hit the 50-rink milestone in 1999–2000.

Most pro leagues played in simultaneously, one season

2: Eddie Shore, Boston and Springfield, 1939–40
Near the end of his legendary NHL career, defenseman Eddie
Shore bought the Springfield Indians of the American Hockey
League. Aware that his presence in the Indians' lineup would be
a terrific drawing card, Shore hammered out an agreement with
his NHL team, the New York Americans, that allowed him to play
for both Springfield and the Americans. In one stretch during
the 1939–40 season, he played eight games in eight nights, com-
muting between various cities to meet his commitments. Shore
was 37 at the time.

Most trading cards of one player

1,215: Wayne Gretzky, 1979–80 to 1998–99
There are no firm stats but according to the *Financial Post*
in December 2000, there were a record 1,215 Gretzky cards
auctioned on eBay's Web site.

Most trading cards owned by a player

85,000: Patrick Roy, 1984–85 to 2001–02
A longtime collector of hockey cards, Roy has amassed a collec-
tion in the vicinity of 85,000. They date back to the early 1900s.

Most appearances by a player on *Sports Illustrated* cover

16: Wayne Gretzky, 1979–80 to 1998–99

The Great One graced 12 exclusive covers and four shared covers of *SI*. When Gretzky retired, he was eighth on the list of all-time cover subjects.

Most appearances by a player on *The Hockey News* cover

70: Wayne Gretzky, 1979–80 to 1998–99

Gretzky always said he made a lot of people a lot of money. He sold a lot of magazines too.

Largest audience for a regular-season game on CBC's *Hockey Night in Canada*

2.16–2.81-million viewers: Wayne Gretzky's final game, April 18, 1999

Most risqué double-entendres by a hockey commentator

Tom Larscheid, CKNW Radio, Vancouver

Tom Larscheid is infamous for his on-air bloopers, many of which have a distinctly homoerotic theme. Some gems include: "Kirk McLean is so fundamentally sound. Look at how erect he is in the net." "There's Sather, with that grin on his face, relaxing behind the bench, hands in his pockets, enjoying himself." And who could forget Larscheid's homage to the Russian Rocket? "Pavel Bure plays with such speed that his linemates can't keep up to him. If only he could play with himself out there, that would really give the fans a show."

Most senior hockey reporter

Red Fisher, The Montreal Gazette

Fisher, the dean of hockey journalism, was born in the same year the NHL took sole possession of the Stanley Cup in 1926. He has been reporting since March 17, 1955, the night of his first assignment: the Maurice Richard Riot in Montreal.

CHAPTER 2

Dress
code

Hockey was one of the first team sports to have its players wear uniform numbers. As early as 1911–12, teams in the Pacific Coast Hockey Association sported digits one through 15 on their jerseys. When the NHL was formed in 1917, it adopted a similar dress code and, later, stipulated that player numbers be placed on skates and the sleeves of uniforms.

Lowest uniform number by a position player

0: Neil Sheehy, Hartford, 1987–88

Defying explanation, the defenseman wore No. 0 for 26 games after he was traded from Calgary to Hartford.

Highest uniform number by a position player

99: Wayne Gretzky, Edmonton, Los Angeles, St. Louis, NY Rangers, 1979–80 to 1998–99

99: Wilf Paiement, Toronto, 1980–81 to 1981–82

99: Rick Dudley, Winnipeg, 1980–81

99: Leo Bourgeault, Joe Lamb, Des Roche, Montreal, 1934–35

Recent NHL rules that prevent players from wearing certain numbers, including triple digits, guarantees this record won't be broken. But No. 99 didn't always command a Wayne Gretzky-like respect. During 1934–35, Montreal issued double-nines to three short-term players. Wilf Paiement and Rick Dudley both tried No. 99 before seeking a less conspicuous number.

Lowest uniform number by a goaltender

0: Paul Bibeault, Montreal, 1942–43

00: John Davidson, NY Rangers, 1975–76

00: Martin Biron, Buffalo, 1995–96

Few goalies have donned as many jersey numbers in as few years as Bibeault. Besides wearing No. 0 in 1942–43, during his 102-game tenure with Montreal, he also wore No. 1, 14, 16 and 21. Davidson tried double-zeroes because teammates Phil Esposito and Ken Hodge sported No. 77 and No. 88. Biron might as well have worn double-zeroes for the anonymity he experienced backing up Dominik Hasek during the Czech's wonder years in Buffalo.

Highest uniform number by a goaltender

No. 93: Darren Puppa, Tampa Bay, 1993–94 to 1999–2000

Puppa wore No. 93 to break with tradition and celebrate the year of his move to the Lightning.

Most frequently retired uniform number
No. 7: retired by eight different teams

For Phil Esposito (Boston), Rick Martin (Buffalo), Neal Broten (Dallas), Ted Lindsay (Detroit), Howie Morenz (Montreal), Rod Gilbert (NY Rangers), Bill Barber (Philadelphia) and Yvon Labre (Washington). Tim Horton and King Clancy's No. 7 is honoured as opposed to retired by the Maple Leafs.

Longest wait to retire a player's number

58 years: Frank Finnigan, Ottawa, 1933–34

Finnigan played his last game for Ottawa in March 1934. The Senators retired his No. 8 prior to the reborn franchise's first game, on October 8, 1992. The 88-year-old Finnigan was on hand for the ceremony.

Shortest career of a player whose number is retired

76 games: Michel Briere, Pittsburgh, 1969–70

After an impressive rookie campaign, Briere appeared destined for a bright career. It was not to be. After suffering severe head injuries in a 1970 car accident, Briere died on April 13, 1971. Although no one was allowed to wear Briere's No. 21 after his death, Pittsburgh did not officially retire the number until January 5, 2001.

Only uniform number retired league-wide by the NHL
No. 99: Wayne Gretzky, 1979–80 to 1998–99

NHL teams that retired uniform numbers of an entire scoring line
Detroit Red Wings: The Production Line
Buffalo Sabres: The French Connection
Detroit retired Gordie Howe's No. 9, Ted Lindsay's No. 7 and Sid
Abel's No. 12. Buffalo retired Gilbert Perreault's No. 11, Rick
Martin's No. 7 and Rene Robert's No. 14.

**Only player to change his uniform number because of a
baby's weight**
Maurice Richard, Montreal, 1943–44
The Rocket initially wore No. 15 when he joined the Canadiens.
He made the switch to No. 9 in his second season to honour his
firstborn child, Huguette, a daughter who weighed nine pounds.

Only player to change his uniform number to get a bigger bed
Gordie Howe, Detroit, 1946–47
When Howe broke in with the Red Wings in 1946–47, he had
No. 17. He switched to No. 9 to improve his sleeping arrangements.
In Howe's day, players were allotted berths on trains during road
trips according to their sweater numbers, and the lower berths
were bigger. Being a big guy, Howe wanted a larger bed.

**Most different uniform numbers worn for an extended period of
time for one team by a Hall of Famer, career**
3: Bobby Hull, Chicago, 1957–58 to 1971–72
The Golden Jet donned three different digits in his 15 years in
Chicago. He began with No. 16, then switched to No. 7, and
finally adopted No. 9 which was the numeral that the
Blackhawks retired in his honour.

CHAPTER 3

Lighting
the lamp

Wayne Gretzky had the kind of career no one imagined was possible. He set standards—many of which will never be broken—in every scoring category. Sniper Marcel Dionne once said, "There's a record book for Wayne Gretzky and one for everyone else in the league." In this chapter, we spread the glory around.

Highest percentage of team's total goals, one season

OLD-TIME RECORD

42.9%: Joe Malone, Quebec Bulldogs, 1919–20

Malone scored 39 of 91 goals by Quebec.

MODERN-DAY RECORD

29.5%: Pavel Bure, Florida, 2000–01

The Pavel Bure-Florida Panthers experiment generated break-away excitement for a few seasons, but ultimately failed when the talent-poor team couldn't find the players to complement Bure's finesse game. The Russian Rocket scored 59 of Florida's 200 goals in 2000–01.

Highest percentage of team's total offense by a player, one season (min. 70 games)

57.3%: Mario Lemieux, Pittsburgh, 1988–89

52.7%: Mario Lemieux, Pittsburgh, 1987–88

51.9%: Wayne Gretzky, Edmonton, 1984–85

Ranked third behind Calgary and Los Angeles in offense during 1988–89, Pittsburgh's 347 goals were due largely to Lemieux, who figured in on 199 of them with 85 goals and 114 assists.

Most points by a player who played only one NHL season (since 1967)

48: Milan Novy, Washington, 1982–83

Washington gambled at the 1982 NHL draft, betting that second-round pick Novy, a Czechoslovakian Player of the Year, would be every bit as good playing the North American game. But the Capitals rolled snake eyes with their 31-year-old rookie. Novy scored 18 goals and 48 points but returned home and never played again in the NHL.

Most goals in a calendar month
20: Teemu Selanne, Winnipeg, 1992–93

The Jets' rookie sensation recorded the NHL's hottest scoring month by a player in March 1993, wiring 20 goals in 14 games, including five power-play goals, two hat tricks, two game-winners, one penalty-shot goal and one empty-net goal. On March 23 he broke Peter Stastny's point record for rookies (109 points) and had an eight-game goal-scoring streak from March 14 to 30 (12 goals).

Most goals by a player in his last season

38: Mike Bossy, NY Islanders, 1986–87
31: Frank Mahovlich, Montreal, 1973–74
28: Darcy Rota, Vancouver, 1983–84
28: Gordie Drillon, Montreal, 1942–43
28: Gerry Heffernan, Montreal, 1943–44
27: Hakan Loob, Calgary, 1988–89

Most points by a player in his last season

85: Hakan Loob, Calgary, 1988–89
80: Frank Mahovlich, Montreal, 1973–74
76: Jean Béliveau, Montreal, 1970–71

Loob played just six NHL seasons, but recorded a 50-goal year in 1987–88 and won the Stanley Cup in 1988–89. Short in stature, Loob was head and shoulders above much of the league in talent. He returned to Sweden in his prime to win three scoring championships and an Olympic gold medal in 1994.

Largest single-season increase in goals (min. 50 games)

39: Owen Nolan, Quebec, 1990–91 to 1991–92

38: Bernie Nicholls, Los Angeles, 1987–88 to 1988–89

37: Wayne Gretzky, Edmonton, 1980–81 to 1981–82

37: Alexander Mogilny, Buffalo, 1991–92 to 1992–93

Nolan jump-started his career with a record-setting 39-goal leap between his three-goal rookie effort in 1990–91 and his 42-goal performance in 1991–92.

Largest single-season decline in goals (min. 50 games)

51: Teemu Selanne, Winnipeg, 1992–93 to 1993–94

41: Charlie Simmer, Los Angeles, 1980–81 to 1981–82

40: Mario Lemieux, Pittsburgh, 1988–89 to 1989–90

37: Jacques Richard, Quebec, 1980–81 to 1981–82

After producing a stratospheric 76 goals in 1992–93, there was only one way to go in Selanne's sophomore season: down. However, the Finnish Flash had a good excuse for his drop to a pedestrian 25 goals in 1993–94: he had his Achilles tendon sliced by a skate blade and played only 51 games.

Largest point increase between two seasons (min. 50 games per season)

72: Bernie Nicholls, Los Angeles, 1987–88 to 1988–89

71: Rob Brown, Pittsburgh, 1987–88 to 1988–89

63: Guy Lafleur, Montreal, 1973–74 to 1974–75

No hockey event had greater impact on Nicholls' career than the Wayne Gretzky trade to the City of Angels in 1988. Nicholls soared from a routine 78-point year to 150 points with Gretzky in 1988–89. Brown got the same booster-rocket effect from playing on a line with Mario Lemieux in 1988–89. He jumped from 44 points to 115.

Largest single-season decline in points (min. 50 games)
78: Teemu Selanne, Winnipeg, 1992–93 to 1993–94
66: Charlie Simmer, Los Angeles, 1980–81 to 1981–82
65: Mark Messier, Edmonton, 1989–90 to 1990–91
Selanne plummeted from 132 points to 54. As mentioned (see page 16), injury played a big part in the drop. Simmer and Messier's declines were more mysterious.

Players with goals in their only NHL game
Rolly Huard, Toronto, December 14, 1930
Huard was called up from the IAHL Buffalo Bisons as an injury replacement. He scored, but it was his only NHL opportunity, a 7–3 loss to Boston.
Dean Morton, Detroit, October 5, 1989
Morton is only the second player in NHL history to notch a goal in his single NHL game. After his 60 minutes in the big show he was back with Detroit's farm team in Adirondack.

Players with goals in all four periods, one game
Bernie Nicholls, Los Angeles, November 13, 1984
Sergei Fedorov, Detroit, December 26, 1996
Nicholls and Fedorov are the only NHLers to score in the first, second, third and overtime periods of one game. Their efforts resulted in 5–4 decisions: Los Angeles defeated Quebec and Detroit beat Washington.

Most goals scored by a player in one overtime
3: Ken Doraty, Toronto, January 16, 1934
By potting an overtime hat trick in a 1933–34 game between Toronto and Ottawa, Doraty set a record that will never be broken. In those days, games tied after regulation were decided

by playing a 10-minute overtime period. There was no sudden-death. Doraty's three goals gave the Maple Leafs a 7–4 victory.

Highest percentage of power-play goals, career (min. 500 goals)
41.3%: Dave Andreychuk, 1982–83 to 2001–02
38.2%: Dino Ciccarelli, 1980–81 to 1998–99
36.9%: Luc Robitaille, 1986–87 to 2001–02
Andreychuk is a power-play shark, feasting on the vulnerability of teams down a man to score a record 245 times in 593 regular-season goals. His numbers top Brett Hull, with 243 power-play markers. (Phil Esposito is credited with 235 power-play goals, but actually counted more. The mark excludes four seasons of Espo's career prior to 1967–68, when the league did not tabulate power-play goals.)

Lowest percentage of power-play goals, career (min. 500 goals)
22.8%: Wayne Gretzky, 1979–80 to 1998–99
25.0%: Jari Kurri, 1980–81 to 1997–98
Gretzky earned his record 894 career goals with the lowest percentage of power-play goals among 500-goal men. He scored 204 times while his team had the man advantage, considerably less than other goal hounds who fattened their counts on the power play, such as Brett Hull (243) and Marcel Dionne (234).

Most shorthanded goals, career
73: Wayne Gretzky, 1979–80 to 1998–99
60: Mark Messier, 1979–80 to 2001–02
Mario Lemieux holds the NHL regular-season record of 13 short-handed goals in 1988–89, but Gretzky is the career leader. Oddly, his official NHL total of 61 records doesn't include this mark, which, considering the speciality of playing shorthanded, deserves recognition.

Highest percentage of game-winning goals scored, career (min. 500 goals)

17.3%: Guy Lafleur, 1971–72 to 1990–91

One of every six goals scored by Lafleur during his illustrious career was a game-winner. His teams—Montreal, NY Rangers and Quebec—won 97 times when he scored one of his 560 career goals. (Only Phil Esposito and Brett Hull have earned their teams more wins with 100 game-winners.)

Highest percentage of power-play goals, one season (min. 30 goals)

71.0%: Marcel Dionne, NY Rangers, 1987–88
68.3%: Dave Andreychuk, Buffalo, 1991–92

The NHL's third-highest career goal scorer, Dionne potted 32 per cent of his 731 career goals on the power play (234 goals), but his career percentage more than doubled during his last complete season, 1987–88, when he scored a record 22 of 31 goals on the power play. In 1991–92, Andreychuk registered 41 goals, 28 on the man-advantage.

Highest percentage of power-play goals by a rookie, one season (min. 30 goals)

60.8%: Joe Nieuwendyk, Calgary, 1987–88

Nieuwendyk's 51 goals in 1987–88 isn't a rookie record but his 31 power-play markers beats all other NHL freshmen with a 61 per cent man-advantage mark.

Highest percentage of shorthanded goals, one season (min. 30 goals)

30.3%: Dirk Graham, Chicago, 1988–89

Graham was a coach's dream on the penalty kill. His puck-savvy defensive work and plowhorse determination forced turnovers

that humiliated the opposition's special teams for 10
shorthanded goals in 33 goals in 1988–89.

Most game-winning goals, one season
16: Phil Esposito, Boston, 1970–71, 76 goals
16: Phil Esposito, Boston, 1971–72, 66 goals
16: Michel Goulet, Quebec, 1983–84, 56 goals
Surprisingly, none of the top three single-season goal scorers—
Wayne Gretzky, Mario Lemieux or Brett Hull—own this mark.
Goulet potted 16 game-winners with the lowest goal count.

Highest percentage of game-winning goals scored, one season (min. 50 goals)
28.6%: Michel Goulet, Quebec, 1983–84
26.0%: Cam Neely, Boston, 1993–1994
25.0%: Peter Bondra, Washington, 1997–1998
This was Goulet's best year. He led the league with 56 goals
and collected 121 points to finish third behind behind Wayne
Gretzky and Mike Bossy. But the real eye-opener was his
16 game-winners for a Nordiques club that won 42 games. In
Goulet's three other 50-goal seasons he never recorded more
than six game-winners. Neely registered 13 game-winners in
50 goals for a Bruins club that won 42 games. Bondra compiled
13 game-winners in 52 goals for the Capitals team that won
40 games.

Lowest percentage of game-winning goals scored, one season (minimum 50 goals)
0%: Mike Bullard, Pittsburgh, 1983–84
Amazingly, not a single one of Bullard's 51 goals won a game for
Pittsburgh. In his defense, he had fewer chances than any other
50-goal man. The cellar-dwelling Penguins won only 16 games.

Most goals without a power-play goal, one season

31: Doug Smail, Winnipeg, 1984–85

28: John Wensink, Boston, 1978–79

27: Stan Jonathan, Boston, 1977–78

Smail forged a career year with 31 goals in 1984–85, the highest total without a man-advantage marker. Wensink and Jonathan, third and fourth liners during Boston's lunch-pail years with coach Don Cherry, earned their goal counts honestly, playing hard-nosed five-on-five hockey.

Fewest power-play goals by a 40-goal scorer

3: Mike Rogers, Hartford, 1979–80

3: Mark Napier, Montreal, 1982–83

Runts of their teams, Rogers and Napier snipped their way to the 40-goal plateau mainly on even-strength play. No one has gone so far in scoring with so few (three) power-play markers. Rogers notched 44 goals and Napier, 40 goals.

Fewest power-play goals by a 50-goal scorer
5: Reggie Leach, Philadelphia, 1979–80

Pat Quinn's first full season behind the bench limited Leach's power-play totals to just five goals. But it worked wonders for his overall goal production as the Riverton Rifle recorded his second-best goal-scoring year in 1979–80.

Most goals by a penalty-minute leader, one season

35: Dave "Tiger" Williams, Vancouver, 1980–81

29: Joe Lamb, Ottawa, 1929–30

29: Bob Probert, Detroit, 1987–88

Because of his physical presence, Williams did pretty much as he pleased. Around the net was no exception, as he set this unofficial goal-scoring record among penalty leaders with 35 goals and 343 minutes in 1980–81.

Most goals by a penalty-free player, one season
28: Bill Mosienko, Chicago, 1944–45
26: Harry Watson, Toronto, 1948–49

Mosienko is best remembered for the NHL's fastest hat trick, an official league record. Unofficially, he holds another mark, scoring a record 28 times during his penalty-free, Lady Byng-winning season of 1944–45.

Most points by a penalty-free player, one season
54: Bill Mosienko, Chicago, 1944–45
54: Clint Smith, Chicago, 1944–45
45: Harry Watson, Toronto, 1948–49

The only time in franchise history that Chicago had more than one regular position player register zero penalty minutes was in 1944–45. That season saw five regulars go penalty free, including Mosienko and Smith, record-holders in this unique category.

Most points by a penalty-minute leader, one season
62: Dave "Tiger" Williams, Vancouver, 1980–81
62: Bob Probert, Detroit, 1987–88

Williams and Probert stockpiled points and penalty minutes with equal flair. For thugs, they had exceptional offensive skills, scoring bigger and badder than any other heavyweights.

Fewest points by a penalty-minute leader, one season
1: Harvey Rockburn, Detroit, 1930–31

Rockburn received a season-high 118 minutes in 1930–31 but

his one assist that year earned him immortality as the lowest-scoring penalty leader in NHL annals.

Most goals by a player traded mid-season

54: Dave Andreychuk, Buffalo to Toronto, 1992–93
Every time Andreychuk touched the puck, it was a potential score. After scoring 29 goals in 52 games in his 11th Buffalo season, Andreychuk was shipped to Toronto where he got another 25 in 31 games. It proved to be Andreychuk's career year and first 50-goal season.

Most goals at time of mid-season trade
34: Mike Gartner, Minnesota to NY Rangers, 1989–90
33: Mark Recchi, Pittsburgh to Philadelphia, 1991–92
Traded for Ulf Dahlen and change, Gartner almost doubled Dahlen's goal production, 34 to 18, at trade time. Gambling that Gartner's best years were behind him, Minnesota got 94 goals from Dahlen over the next three seasons; New York got 145 goals from Gartner.

Most points by a player traded mid-season

112: Bernie Nicholls, Los Angeles to NY Rangers, 1989–90
No one missed Wayne Gretzky more than Nicholls, who scored 75 points before the trade and 37 points with New York. Tomas Sandstrom and Tony Granato went to the Kings.
110: John Cullen, Pittsburgh to Hartford, 1990–91
The big scorers in this six-player trade were Cullen for Ron Francis. Cullen scored 94 points before the swap and 16 later in Hartford. He played 109 games with the Whalers; Francis turned into a major acquisition for the Penguins, playing 533 games.

Most points at time of mid-season trade
94: John Cullen, Pittsburgh to Hartford 1990–91
75: Bernie Nicholls, Los Angeles to NY Rangers, 1989–90

Most goals by two brothers, career
913: Bobby and Dennis Hull, 1950s to 1980s
902: Maurice and Henri Richard, 1940s to 1970s
895: Wayne and Brent Gretzky, 1980s and 1990s

Most goals by a family, career
1,592: Bobby, Dennis and Brett Hull, 1950s to 2000s
Two generations of the Hulls amassed the highest goal count
ever by a family: Bobby had 610 goals, Dennis 303 and Brett
679 as of 2001–02.

Most points by two brothers, career
2,861: Wayne and Brent Gretzky, 1980s and 1990s
2,011: Maurice and Henri Richard, 1940s to 1970s
1,911: Marcel and Gilbert Dionne, 1970s to 1990s

Most points by a family, career
3,070: Bobby, Dennis and Brett Hull, 1950s to 2000s
2,935: Brian, Duane, Darryl, Brent, Rich and Ron Sutter, 1970s to 2000s
The Hulls are the only hockey family ever to break the 3,000-
point plateau in regular-season scoring.

Most goals by two brothers, one season
93: Pavel and Valeri Bure, 1999–2000
88: Bobby and Dennis Hull, 1968–69
The Bures broke a 31-year-old record in 1999–2000. While Pavel
and Bobby each scored 58 times for their respective families, the
difference was Valeri whose 35 goals topped Dennis's total of 30.

Most goals by a family, one season

138: The Sutters, six brothers, 1983–84 and 1984–85

Family size alone cannot account for this record, but it played a large part as the Sutters hit 138 goals in consecutive seasons.

Most goals by two teammates, one season
144: Wayne Gretzky and Jari Kurri, Edmonton, 1984–85

Gretzky and Kurri's 144 goals equalled 40 per cent or more of the total goal production of every NHL team in 1984–85. The one exception was their own team, Edmonton, which scored 401 goals.

Most goals by two defensemen on the same team, one season

64: Bobby Orr and Carol Vadnais, Boston, 1974–75
59: Paul Coffey and Marty McSorley, Edmonton, 1985–86
59: Kevin Hatcher and Al Iafrate, Washington, 1992–93

While the bulk of this record 64-goal total belongs to Orr (46 goals), Vadnais's 18 goals gave the pair this unofficial record.

Most points by two brothers, one season

228: Peter and Marian Stastny, Quebec, 1981–82
216: Peter and Anton Stastny, Quebec, 1982–83

The Stastnys represented a deep talent-pool for the Nordiques. Peter was always the top point-earner among the three, but Marian and Anton both kept pace to produce the top two aggregates ever by brothers.

Most points by a family, one season

316: Brent, Brian, Darryl, Duane, Rich and Ron Sutter, 1984–85

Brent scored 102 points; Brian, 74; Ron, 45; Duane, 41; Darryl, 38; and Rich, 16.

Most points by two teammates, one season

353: Wayne Gretzky and Paul Coffey, Edmonton, 1985–86
343: Wayne Gretzky and Jari Kurri, Edmonton, 1984–85

Few duos could approach the 353 points Gretzky and Coffey stockpiled in 1985–86, when each had career years of 215 and 138 points. The exception would be another Gretzky duo.

Most points by two defensemen on the same team, one season

209: Bobby Orr and Carol Vadnais, Boston, 1974–75
184: Bobby Orr and Dallas Smith, 1970–71

Orr scored 135 points and won the NHL scoring race but Vadnais also had his personal-best year, netting 74 points. (Besides Orr the only other rearguard to top Vadnais in 1974–75 was Denis Potvin with 76 points.)

Most goals by two brothers, one game

7: Peter and Anton Stastny, Quebec, February 22, 1981

Peter scored four goals and Anton added three in an 11–7 victory over Washington.

Most goals by two opposing defensemen, one game

8: Hap Day and John McKinnon, November 19, 1929

Toronto's Day and Pittsburgh's McKinnon each scored four goals in a 10–5 Pirates' win.

Most points by two brothers, one game

16: Peter and Anton Stastny, Quebec, February 22, 1981

The Stastnys share the official NHL record for most points in one road game, but their genealogy affords them another mark as top point-scoring brothers in one game. Peter and Anton each netted eight points against Washington in an 11–7 win by Quebec. They were both NHL rookies at the time.

CHAPTER 4

Star-
crossed stars

Not every established NHL star holds an offensive mark worthy of star status—at least not according to our records book. For example, despite an exemplary 500-goal career, Ron Francis rates the highest career goal count without ever achieving the rank of a 40-goal scorer. Conversely, not every NHL offensive record elevates a player to star status. Remember the name Guy Charron.

Most goals without winning the scoring title, career

708: Mike Gartner, 1979–80 to 1997–98

Gartner ranks fifth among hockey's greatest all-time goal-scorers, but unlike his colleagues in the top five, he never led the NHL in points. He never led in goals either.

Most points without winning the scoring title, career
1,804: Mark Messier, 1979–80 to 2001–02

Somebody stop this man. Without ever winning a scoring title, Messier is on the verge of passing Howe's 1,850 career points for second place on the all-time point leaders. Messier is the first NHLer since Gordie Howe in 1979–80 to play 23 seasons.

Most goals without a 30-goal season, career

324: Al MacInnis, 1983–84 to 2001–02
323: Dale Hunter, 1980–81 to 1998–99

Considering the wicked velocity of his shot, one might expect MacInnis to have hit 30 goals in one season during his career. The closest he got was 28 in 1989–1990 and 1990–91 with Calgary. Hunter reached 28 in 1985–86 and 1991–92 with Washington.

Fewest goals among 30-goal players, career

33: Tom Webster, 1968–69 to 1979–80
39: Ken Hodge Jr., 1988–89 to 1992–93

Webster scored 30 goals with Detroit in 1970–71 before injuries limited his play. He moved to the WHA, netting 220 goals over six seasons. Second-place Hodge scored a 30-goal rookie season with Boston, then fell off the radar.

Most goals without a 50-goal season, career

801: Gordie Howe, 1946–47 to 1979–80

Howe built the NHL's highest goal count of his era without ever attaining the 50-goal mark. He came very close, scoring 49 in 1952–53.

Fewest goals among 50-goal players, career

160: Jacques Richard, 1972–73 to 1982–83

192: Wayne Babych, 1978–79 to 1986–87

193: Hakan Loob, 1983–84 to 1988–89

Richard scored 52 goals with Quebec; and Babych, 54 goals with St. Louis. Loob rates third with probably the most skills of the three. He scored 50 goals with Calgary in 1987–88.

Most points without a 100-point season, career

1,579: Ray Bourque, 1979–80 to 2000–01

1,467: Stan Mikita, 1958–59 to 1979–80

Bourque could have sacrificed his defensive game for the scoresheet and reached the 100-point mark. But his career plus-528 proves he never forgot his own zone. Bourque's best year was a 95-point effort in 1986–87. Mikita posted career highs of 97 points twice.

Fewest points among 100-point players, career

347: Jacques Richard, 1972–73 to 1982–83

Richard was always a defensive liability but, with the right line-mates, clubs could overlook his minus totals hoping for one big season. Richard got it in Quebec. Teamed with the Stastnys he scored 103 points in 1980–81, almost 30 per cent of his 10-year career output.

500-goal players without a 50-goal season

PLAYER	TEAMS	SEASONS	GOALS
Gordie Howe	Det, Htf	1946–1980	801
Stan Mikita	Chicago	1958–1980	541
Frank Mahovlich	Tor, Det, Mon	1956–1974	533
Pat Verbeek	NJ, Htf, NYR, Dal, Det	1982–2002	522
Ron Francis	Htf, Pitt, Carolina	1981–2002	514
Gilbert Perreault	Buffalo	1970–1987	512
Jean Béliveau	Montreal	1950–1971	507

Fewest goals short of a 500th goal by a retired player

2: Glenn Anderson, 1980–81 to 1995–96

9: Jean Ratelle, 1960–61 to 1980–81

Anderson played 16 seasons and Ratelle 21, but both needed to play one more to reach the 500-goal plateau. Anderson scored 498 career goals; Ratelle 491. (Who scored the fewest goals above 500? Lanny McDonald hit 500 on the nose and Joe Mullen potted 502.)

Fewest points short of a 1,000th point by a retired player

12: Rick Middleton, 1974–75 to 1987–88

14: Dave Keon, 1960–61 to 1981–82

Middleton's 14 NHL seasons left him 12 points shy of the milestone, with 988 points. Keon had 986 points in 18 years. (Who scored the fewest points above the 1,000-point mark? Brian Propp picked up 1,004 points in 1,016 games; and Lanny McDonald, who had a knack for reaching the ultimate prize in the nick of time, scored 1,006 points in 1,111 games.)

Most goals without winning the scoring title, one season

86: Brett Hull, St. Louis, 1990–91

Hull scored 35 goals more than his closest rivals in 1990–91 and easily doubled points leader Wayne Gretzky's 41-goal count. But Gretzky almost tripled Hull in assists, 122 to 45, which gave the Great One another scoring title with 163 points to Hull's 131.

Most goals without winning the goal-scoring title, one season

71: Jari Kurri, Edmonton, 1984–85
70: Bernie Nicholls, Los Angeles, 1988–89

Not surprisingly, both Kurri and Nicholls were linemates with Wayne Gretzky at the time of their greatest offensive outputs.

Most points without winning the scoring title, one season

168: Wayne Gretzky, Los Angeles, 1988–89
155: Steve Yzerman, Detroit, 1988–89
150: Bernie Nicholls, Los Angeles, 1988–89

Who let the dogs out? This was the only season in history in which four players reached the 150-point mark. For Mario Lemieux (who led the league with 199 points), Yzerman and Nicholls, their totals represented career highs.

Most goals without an assist, one season

13: John McKinnon, Pittsburgh Pirates, 1926–27

The NHL statkeepers may have had something to do with this— assists were handed out sparingly in 1926–27. Even so, how does an obscure defenseman like McKinnon end up with this mark? We think it extremely unlikely this one will fall.

Most points without a goal, one season

29: Jimmy Thomson, Toronto, 1947–48

27: Barry Wilkins, Pittsburgh, 1975–76

Thomson was one of the great clutch-and-grab defensemen of his era. He scored only 19 goals in 787 games, but assisted on 215 which included three seasons of 20 assists or more without a goal. His NHL-record 29 assists was impressive considering he played only 59 games and the league's top set-up man, Doug Bentley, had 37.

Most goals without winning the game

5: Alexei Zhamnov, Winnipeg, April 1, 1995

Zhamnov is the only NHLer ever to score five goals or more in a game without being rewarded with a win by his team. Winnipeg's 7–7 tie against Los Angeles ranks as hockey's worst unintentional April Fool's joke by teammates on a player.

Most goals without a playoff appearance, career

221: Guy Charron, 1969–70 to 1980–81

Guy Charron was snakebit. Good enough to play 734 games, Charron missed the playoffs in all 12 seasons with Detroit, Kansas City, Washington and the 1969–70 Montreal Canadiens, the only Habs team to miss the playoffs in almost a half-century (1948 to 1995).

Most points without a playoff appearance, career

530: Guy Charron, 1969–70 to 1980–81

Unfortunately, Charron leads the league in all offensive marks in this category, goals (221), assists (309) and points (530).

Most goals by a player on a non-playoff team, one season

70: Mario Lemieux, Pittsburgh, 1987–88

62: Steve Yzerman, Detroit, 1989–90

The NHL is riddled with stories and stats of great individual efforts spoiled by team ineptitude. None of these are represented better than Lemieux's sparkling 70-goal season on the Patrick Division's cellar-dwelling Penguins.

Most points by a player on a non-playoff team, one season

168: Mario Lemieux, Pittsburgh, 1987–88
136: Denis Maruk, Washington, 1981–82
127: Steve Yzerman, Detroit, 1989–90

Lemieux holds a number of NHL scoring marks, including a few unofficial records of futility. One of his least known may be his first scoring championship in 1987–88, as Pittsburgh fell to last place with 81 points in the Patrick Division.

Most goals by a player never voted an NHL All-Star, career

708: Mike Gartner, 1979–80 to 1997–98

Despite a lethal scoring touch from the right wing, Gartner was never voted to either a first or second All-Star team in his 19-year career.

Most goals by a player who never played in an NHL All-Star game, career

397: Steve Thomas, 1984–85 to 2001–02

Thomas' intensity and speed carried him a long way but not far enough for an All-Star game invite. Still, his career goal production tops all other non-All-Stars.

Most points by a player never voted an NHL All-Star, career

1,701: Ron Francis, 1981–82 to 2001–02

Every time Francis earned a potential All-Star berth after a 100-point year, other star centres besides Gretzky and Lemieux would edge him out in the All-Star balloting; players such as Mark Messier, Pat LaFontaine and Eric Lindros.

Most points by a player who never played in an NHL All-Star game, career

881: Steve Thomas, 1984–85 to 2001–02

Despite his reputation as a B playmaker, Thomas had four 100-point seasons. His 881-point total never took him within a whiff of an All-Star opportunity. It's a distinction worthy of an unofficial record.

Most games by a player who never played in an NHL All-Star game, career

1,318: Guy Carbonneau, 1980–81 to 1999–2000

Defensive specialists are often overlooked when they hand out invitations to the mid-season shindig. Despite winning three Selke Trophies as the league's top defensive forward, Carbonneau never skated in an All-Star game during his 19-year career.

Most goals by a player not voted an NHL All-Star, one season

70: Bernie Nicholls, Los Angeles, 1988–89

Nicholls suffered the same fate as many centres (such as Ron Francis) during the Wayne Gretzky-Mario Lemieux era. Even though he scored a career-high 70 goals, Lemieux (85 goals) and Gretzky (54 goals) were chosen first and second All-Star centres.

Most points by a player not voted an NHL All-Star, one season

155: Steve Yzerman, Detroit, 1988–89

Yzerman's career year of 155 points was good enough for third in the scoring race, but guess who finished first and second? Mario Lemieux (199 points) and Wayne Gretzky (168 points). They nabbed the first and second All-Star centre slots.

CHAPTER 5

Jock
of ages

In a 1979 game against Edmonton, Gordie Howe of the Hartford Whalers scored on his first shift to celebrate the birth of his son Mark's firstborn child: Travis Howe. On that evening Howe became the only grandfather to score in an NHL game. Mr. Methuselah was 51 years old and playing in his 32nd season of professional hockey.

Age of the youngest player in an NHL game

16.11 years: Bep Guidolin, Boston, 1942–43

A wartime replacement player, Guidolin was pressed into service with Boston on November 12, 1942, just one month shy of his 17th birthday.

Age of the oldest player in an NHL game

52 years: Gordie Howe, Hartford, 1979–80

Mr. Hockey retired at age 52 on April 11, 1980. He played 32 seasons of pro hockey during a career that spanned five decades.

Age of the oldest player to make his debut in an NHL game

ALL-TIME RECORD

41 years: Hugh Lehman, Chicago, 1926–27

Lehman was a long-time pro goalie on western teams, most notably with the Vancouver Millionaires when he won a Stanley Cup in 1915. His first NHL game came on November 17, 1926.

MODERN-DAY RECORD

38.3 years: Connie Madigan, St. Louis, 1972–73

Often cited as the league's oldest rookie, Madigan had an extensive minor-league career, but played only 20 NHL games, his first on February 6, 1973.

Age of the youngest goalie

17.1 years: Harry Lumley, Detroit, 1943–44
18.1 years: Olivier Michaud, Montreal, 2001–2002

Lumley was brought up from the minors for a two-game tryout by Detroit. He lost his first game 6–2 to the Rangers on December 19, 1943. Oddly, Lumley also played for the Rangers during his brief stay that year, when Detroit loaned him to New York for one game to replace injured Ken McAuley. That earned Lumley another distinction: the youngest goalie to play for two NHL teams.

Age of the oldest goalie

45.11 years: Moe Roberts, Chicago, 1951–52
45.1 years: Johnny Bower, Toronto, 1969–70

This record has Bower written all over it. He backstopped more games than any other netminder in professional hockey. His nickname, "China Wall" was a tribute as much to his age and endurance as to his play. He was hockey's great warhorse, playing 20 games in 1968–69 and one final match at age 45 on December 10, 1969, a 6–3 loss to Montreal. However, the title for oldest goalie belongs to Moe Roberts, a career minor leaguer, who played just 10 NHL games. Roberts was almost 46 years old when he replaced injured Harry Lumley in a 5–2 loss against Detroit on November 25, 1951. He hadn't played a pro game in five seasons.

Age of the youngest first overall draft pick
17.10 years: Pierre Turgeon, Granby Bisons, 1986–87

Turgeon lit up the junior ranks in his last season with Granby where he scored 154 points in 58 games. He wasn't even 18 when the NHL came calling. The Buffalo Sabres made him their first overall pick in 1987.

Age of the oldest draft pick

37 years: Helmut Balderis

Balderis, a Soviet scoring champion during the 1970s and early 1980s, retired in 1985 but was lured back to hockey after being selected 13th, 238th overall by Minnesota in 1989. Clearly Balderis's expiry date was up. The aging Latvian lasted just 26 games in the NHL.

Age of the oldest draft pick chosen first overall

20.5 years: Rob Ramage, WHA Birmingham Bulls, 1978–79
Ramage signed as an underage free agent with Birmingham
in 1978, played one WHA season before the league folded
and then was drafted by the Colorado Rockies first overall
in 1979.

Age of the youngest team captain
19.2 years: Brian Bellows, Minnesota, 1983–84
19.11 years: Vincent Lecavalier, Tampa Bay, 1999–2000
The only two teenage captains in NHL annals. Bellows, a mere year
out of the junior ranks, was named the North Stars' co-captain on
an interim basis when captain Craig Hartsburg went down two
games into the 1983–84 season with a knee injury. Lecavalier
became Tampa's captain on March 10, 2000.

Age of the youngest player to score five goals in a game

19.11 years: Don Murdoch, NY Rangers, October 12, 1976
20.0 years: Wayne Gretzky, Edmonton, February 18, 1981
The Rangers rookie was two weeks shy of turning 20 and in only
his fourth NHL game when he blitzed goalie Gary Smith for five
goals in a 10–4 massacre of the Minnesota North Stars.

Age of the oldest player to score five goals in a game

32.8 years: Syd Howe, Detroit, February 3, 1944
32.5 years: Punch Broadbent, Montreal Maroons, January 7, 1925
Before Gordie there was Syd. Although the two players were not
related, they both starred for Detroit. Howe actually scored six
times as the Red Wings thumped the hapless Rangers and goalie
Ken McAuley by a 12–2 margin.

Age of the youngest 50-goal player

19.2 years: Wayne Gretzky, Edmonton, 1979–80
19.8 years: Jimmy Carson, Los Angeles, 1987–88
Gretzky and Carson are linked in more ways than just their
Edmonton-Los Angeles trade. Months before the famous deal,
Carson potted his 50th to join the Great One as the only other
teenage 50-goal scorer. Gretzky's 50th came in his 78th NHL game
on April 2, 1980; Carson got his in his 157th game on March 26, 1988.

Age of the oldest 50-goal player

35.10 years: Johnny Bucyk, Boston, 1970–71
Like fine wine, Bucyk got better as he aged. He didn't reach the
milestone until his 16th season, in his 1,041st career game on
March 16, 1971. The Bruins left-winger played seven more seasons.

Age of the youngest 100-point player

18.11 years: Dale Hawerchuk, Winnipeg, 1981–82
Hawerchuk was an immediate success in the NHL, scoring
point No. 100 in his 74th career game on March 24, 1982. His
103-point year earned him the Calder Trophy as top rookie and
it was the second-highest points total by a rookie up to that
time in league history.

Age of the oldest 100-point player

41.0 years: Gordie Howe, Detroit, 1968–69
Mr. Hockey recorded only one 100-point season during his 26-
year NHL career. He reached the milestone in his 1,548th career
game on March 30, 1969.

Age of the youngest 500-goal player

25.10 years: Wayne Gretzky, Edmonton, 1986–87
In only his 575th NHL game, Gretzky netted his 500th goal,

almost 400 games faster than the 972-game average for 500-goal scorers. Gretzky's 500th was scored on November 22, 1986.

Age of the oldest 500-goal player

40.5 years: Johnny Bucyk, Boston, 1975–76
Playing hockey longer than some of his teammates had been alive, Bucyk scored No. 500 in his 21st season. It came on October 30, 1975.

Age of the youngest 1,000-point player

23.11 years: Wayne Gretzky, Edmonton, 1984–85
26.5 years: Mario Lemieux, Pittsburgh, 1991–92
Gretzky posted his 1,000th point on December 19, 1984; Lemieux notched his on March 24, 1992.

Age of the oldest 1,000-point player

37.10 years: Henri Richard, Montreal, 1973–74
37.6 years: Dale Hunter, Washington, 1997–98
A veteran of 11 Stanley Cups, Richard finally reached point No. 1,000 in his 19th season on December 20, 1973. Hunter hit the mark on January 9, 1998.

Age of the youngest goalie to record 300 wins

29.6 years: Martin Brodeur, New Jersey, 2001–02
Brodeur reached the milestone with a 2–0 shutout of Ottawa on December 15, 2001. If he continues at his current pace and has a lengthy career, he could one day challenge Patrick Roy as the NHL's leader in career wins.

Age of the youngest goalie to record 400 wins

33.4 years: Patrick Roy, Colorado, 1998–99
On February 5, 1999, Roy claimed his 400th win in a 3–1 decision

against Detroit, the team Terry Sawchuk—the next-youngest 400-win goalie at 35 years—played with for much of his career.

Age of the oldest goalie to record 400 wins
42.1 years: Jacques Plante, Toronto, 1970–71

Only six goalies have broken the 400-win mark. Plante, the most senior, played 756 games to reach the milestone in an 8–1 win against Los Angeles on February 13, 1971.

Age of the oldest leader in goals-against average, one season (min. 40 games)
42.3 years: Jacques Plante, Toronto, 1970–71

Years past the average age of most NHL retirees, Plante allowed just 73 goals in 40 games to lead the NHL with a 1.88 GAA. It was Plante's ninth occasion to lead the league in goals against.

Age of the youngest scoring champion
20.3 years: Wayne Gretzky, Edmonton, 1980–81

In only his second NHL season, Gretzky scored 164 points to win the scoring championship. He didn't relinquish the title for another seven years.

Age of the oldest scoring champion
36.5 years: Bill Cook, NY Rangers, 1932–33

Cook had been a scoring leader in the pro western leagues before they folded into the NHL in 1926. The 30-year-old veteran won the scoring title in his rookie NHL season, 1926–27, and won it again as the oldest scoring leader in NHL history when he posted 50 points at age 36 in 1932–33.

Age of the youngest MVP

19.5 years: Wayne Gretzky, Edmonton, 1979–80

When Gretzky won the Hart Trophy as MVP in his first season, it marked the first time in more than a half century of hockey that a freshman took home the coveted award. Herb Gardiner of Montreal won the Hart in his first NHL season in 1926–27.

Age of the oldest MVP

35.11 years: Herb Gardiner, Montreal, 1926–27

Already a star defenseman in the Western Hockey League, Gardiner moved east in 1926–27 and quickly established himself as one of the NHL's top defensemen, becoming the first rearguard to win the Hart Trophy. In more than 70 years, no one has surpassed his age as an MVP winner.

Age of the youngest Norris Trophy winner

20.2 years: Bobby Orr, Boston, 1967–68
21.2 years: Bobby Orr, Boston, 1968–69

Light years ahead of everyone else in hockey skill development, Orr won his first of eight consecutive Norris Trophies at age 20, in his second NHL season.

Age of the oldest Norris Trophy winner

37.5 years: Doug Harvey, NY Rangers, 1961–62
35.11 years: Al MacInnis, St. Louis, 1998–99

Harvey's Norris with the Rangers was his seventh in eight seasons. He won as a player-coach, the only Norris winner who can claim that distinction.

Age of the youngest Vezina Trophy winner

19.3 years: Tom Barrasso, Buffalo, 1983–84

Barrasso finished high school at age 18 and within the year

had dazzled the NHL, winning both the Vezina Trophy as top goaltender and the Calder Trophy as best rookie. At the time, only two other netminders—Frank Brimsek and Tony Esposito—had been so honoured in the same season. Brimsek was 23 and Esposito was 27.

Age of the oldest Vezina Trophy winner

40.6 years: Johnny Bower, Toronto, 1964–65
40.3 years: Jacques Plante, St. Louis, 1968–69
Few nicknames suited a goalie better than the China Wall for Bower. He was old, durable and stopped hordes of invaders during his time.

Age of the oldest penalty-minutes leader

36.10 years: Joe Hall, Montreal, 1918–19
33.7 years: Red Dutton, NY Americans, 1931–32
33.7 years: Ted Lindsay, Chicago, 1958–59
Time did not mellow "Bad" Joe Hall. The scrappy Canadiens defenseman led the NHL in penalty minutes in both 1917–18 and 1918–19 at the ages of 35 and 36. Hall did not live to see 37. He died in the infleunza epidemic of 1919. Lindsay took a run at Hall's record in 1964–65. Returning to the NHL after four years in retirement, the 39-year-old warhorse collected 173 PIM, only four minutes behind Carl Brewer's league-leading total.

Age of the youngest player to appear in NHL All-Star game

18.5 years: Fleming MacKell, Toronto, 1947
An outstanding junior with St. Michael's College, MacKell was invited to play with Toronto against the NHL All-Stars at the 1947 contest. He was just 18 and still hadn't played a single NHL game. During that era, the All-Star game pitted the defending Cup champion against a squad of All-Stars.

Age of the youngest player inducted into the Hall of Fame

31 years: Bobby Orr, 1966–67 to 1977–78

32 years: Mario Lemieux, 1984–85 to 2001–02

Both superstars were admitted without the Hall's mandatory
three-year waiting period. They were honoured in the year they
retired: Orr in 1979 and Lemieux in 1997. Maybe Lemieux
thought he was too young to be enshrined. He returned to
action in 2000–01.

Age of the youngest NHL head coach

26.1 years: Gary Green, Washington, 1979–80

27.8 years: Eddie Gerard, Ottawa, 1917–18

28.5 years: Lionel Conacher, NY Americans, 1929–30

Green, already a Memorial Cup-winning coach with the OHL Peter-
borough Petes, had been coaching the Capitals farm team in
Hershey for only a month when he took over from Danny Belisle as
Washington's new bench boss. In 157 career games, Green logged
a 50–78–29 record.

Age of the oldest NHL head coach

68.9 years: Scotty Bowman, Detroit, 2001–02

Bowman is a Biblical figure. Roger Neilson coached two Ottawa
games in 2001–02 to reach the 1,000-game plateau. He was 67.

CHAPTER 6

Boon
or bust

Few NHL teams, expansion or
otherwise, have delivered a worst
performance or established more unwanted records
in a regular-season schedule than the Washington
Capitals of 1974–75. Their sum, unfortunately, was
no greater than their parts. As individuals, the
Capitals took home a few unsavoury records of their
own, notably in the plus-minus column. (Plus-
minus figures are only available from 1967–68.)

Most consecutive plus seasons

20: Larry Robinson, 1972–73 to 1991–92

18: Al MacInnis, 1981–82 to 2001–02

17: Ray Bourque, 1979–80 to 2000–01

During his 20-year career, Robinson never recorded a minus season, a perfect 20 for 20 score; MacInnis is on the fast track, passing Bourque with his 18th plus season in 2001–02; and Bourque finally succumbed to a minus-11 in his 18th season, 1996–97, when Boston finished dead last in the standings.

Most consecutive seasons leading plus-minus totals
4: Bobby Orr, 1966–67 to 1978–79

The only NHLer to lead in more than two consecutive seasons is Orr, who had the best plus numbers four straight years and six overall.

Highest plus-minus, career (min. 500 games)

Plus-730: Larry Robinson, 1972–73 to 1991–92

Plus-617: Bobby Orr, 1966–67 to 1978–79

Plus-528: Ray Bourque, 1979–80 to 2000–01

Plus-518: Wayne Gretzky, 1979–80 to 1998–99

Robinson's big lead is partly a product of playing for so many great Montreal teams. Even so, none of his Canadiens teammates rank anywhere close to him. Orr's total would be much higher if his career had not been shortened by injury. Orr played 657 games. Robinson played 1,384.

Highest plus-minus, one season

Plus-124: Bobby Orr, Boston, 1970–71

Plus-120: Larry Robinson, Montreal, 1976–77

Defensemen for all ages, Orr and Robinson played both sides of the blueline equally well, although Orr's offensive skills were unequalled. Both won the Norris Trophy as top rearguards.

Lowest plus-minus, one season

Minus-82: Bill Mikkelson, Washington, 1974–75

Washington fans were ready to inflict Capital punishment after suffering through 1974–75's expansion season of 8–67–5. Not one regular player recorded a plus season in the record 446 goals against Washington. The worst plus-minus befell defenseman Bill Mikkelson, who set an NHL standard of minus-82. The ugly numbers: Mikkelson was on the ice for 156 of the 446 goals against Washington and only 45 of 181 goals for.

Highest plus-minus by a forward, one season

Plus-98: Wayne Gretzky, Edmonton, 1984–85
Plus-89: Guy Lafleur, Montreal, 1976–77
Plus-88: Steve Shutt, Montreal, 1976–77

Gretzky was on the ice for 249 Edmonton goals (73 were his) and 127 goals against. Subtract power-play goals for and against and the Great One owns this exclusive record.

Lowest plus-minus by a forward, one season

Minus-65: Mike Marson, Washington, 1974–75

What happened to Marson is the same story of a number of good players who were drafted high out of junior hockey to expansion teams in the 1960s and 1970s. They weren't ready or they were over-worked and not given a real opportunity to develop. In Marson's case, he stepped from the cosy confines of the OHL Sudbury Wolves (where he scored 94 points in 69 games in 1973–74) into the debacle of Washington's first season. Not one Capitals player escaped 1974–75 with a plus total. Unfortunately, the Scarborough, Ontario, native with 28 points hit the skids and recorded the worst plus-minus ever by a forward, a minus-65.

Lowest plus-minus by a scoring champion
Minus-25: Wayne Gretzky, Los Angeles, 1993–94
Gretzky scored a league-high 130 points while recording his personal-worst plus-minus of his career at minus-25.

Highest plus-minus by a scoring champion
Plus-98: Wayne Gretzky, Edmonton, 1984–85
With few exceptions (such as Stan Mikita, see page 58), NHLers rarely hold both the best and worst marks in an individual record. Include Gretzky in this category. To offset his record low of minus-25 by a scoring leader, the Great One compiled a career-high plus-98 during his 208-point campaign in 1984–85.

Lowest plus-minus by a 50-goal player
Minus-33: Mike Bullard, Pittsburgh, 1983–84
Bullard's 51 goals didn't help him avoid setting this unwanted record. He was playing with Pittsburgh after all, league cellar-dwellers with 136 more goals allowed than scored.
Minus-22: Rick Martin, Buffalo, 1973–74
Martin scored 52 goals on the sub-.500 Sabres.

Lowest plus-minus by 100-point players
Minus-40: Joe Sakic, Quebec, 1989–90
Minus-35: Mario Lemieux, Pittsburgh, 1984–85
Minus-31: Michel Goulet, Quebec, 1987–88

Lowest plus-minus by 100-point defensemen

Minus-25: Paul Coffey, Pittsburgh, 1989–90

Minus-10: Paul Coffey, Pittsburgh, 1988–89

Coffey is hockey's second-most gifted offensive defenseman, but as Penguins general manager Craig Patrick found out, make sure he has backup. Coffey was in the plus column much of his career, except in Steeltown where he accomplished this unofficial record of a minus-25 and a minus-10, while scoring 103 and 113 points in 1989–90 and 1988–89.

Lowest plus-minus by a Norris Trophy winner (top defenseman)

Minus-16: Randy Carlyle, Pittsburgh, 1980–81

Minus-3: Rob Blake, Los Angeles, 1997–98

Since plus-minus totals were first tabulated in 1967–68, only two defensemen with minus totals have won the Norris.

Highest plus-minus by a Selke Trophy winner (top defensive forward)

Plus-49: Sergei Fedorov, Detroit, 1993–94

Plus-48: Sergei Fedorov, Detroit, 1995–96

Plus-47: Dave Poulin, Philadelphia, 1986–87

Fedorov is the only Selke winner who could lay claim to being the league's top offensive forward in the same season. In 1993–94, the smooth-skating Russian tallied 120 points, second only to Wayne Gretzky's 130.

Lowest plus-minus by a Selke Trophy winner (top defensive forward)

Minus-18: Steve Kasper, Boston, 1981–82

Minus-2 : Bob Gainey, Montreal, 1979–80

What were the voters smoking? Kasper had the worst plus-minus on the Bruins and Gainey had the second-worst plus-minus on the Canadiens. Gainey won the Selke the first four years it was awarded, yet in year five (1981-82), when he posted a career-high plus-37, the voters inexplicably gave the trophy to Kasper.

Highest plus-minus by a top 50 goal-scoring rookie
Plus-45: Brian Propp, Philadelphia, 1979–80
Plus-44: Steve Larmer, Chicago, 1982–83

Propp's two-way skills were evident from Philadelphia's first faceoff in 1979–80. He scored 34 goals and had an all-time rookie record of plus-45. Chicago was equally fortunate in Larmer, who turned in a 43-goal performance on a plus-44 season.

Highest plus-minus by a rookie

Plus-52: Ray Bourque, Boston, 1979–80
Plus-47: Bill Hajt, Buffalo, 1974–75

They will have to resort to genetic engineering to produce a more polished rookie rearguard than Bourque.

Lowest plus-minus by a rookie

Minus-68: Greg Joly, Washington, 1974–75
Minus-65: Mike Marson, Washington, 1974–75

If you haven't connected the dots yet, this Washington club was a mess. These two rookies never recovered from this beating.

Highest plus-minus, one game

Plus-10: Tom Bladon, Philadelphia, December 11, 1977

Bladon recorded a mind-boggling plus-10 after notching four goals and four assists. Bladon was also on the ice for two other Flyer goals in an 11–1 drubbing of the Cleveland Barons.

CHAPTER 7

No
quarter

Tiger Williams and Dale Hunter sat

in the penalty box longer than any

other NHL players. In 14 seasons Williams elbowed,

cross-checked, speared, whacked and punched his

way to a league record 3,966 minutes, 401 minutes

more than 19-year tough guy Hunter, with

3,565 minutes in career box time. Combined,

Williams and Hunter spent roughly 125 games in

the cooler . . . not including game suspensions.

Most penalty minutes by a scoring champion, career

1,808: Ted Lindsay, 1944–45 to 1964–65
1,685: Gordie Howe, 1946–47 to 1979–80

For anyone who didn't witness Terrible Ted play hockey, this record represents the best evidence of his hockey skills. One of the all-time greatest fighters, Lindsay also regularly finished in the top 10 among scorers. He won the scoring championship in 1949–50 and was inducted into the Hall in 1966. Further proof of Lindsay's ferocity, he even topped the penalty total of Howe, who was no choirboy.

Most penalty minutes by a 500-goal player

2,905: Pat Verbeek, 1982–83 to 2001–02

Affectionately known as the Little Ball of Hate, Verbeek leads all 500-goal scorers in penalties.

Fewest penalty minutes by a 500-goal player

210: Mike Bossy, 1977–78 to 1986–87

A noted pacifist, Bossy averaged one minor every eight games throughout his 10-year career. He scored 573 career goals.

Most penalty minutes by a 1,000-point player

3,565: Dale Hunter, 1980–81 to 1999–2000

Hunter's 1,020 career points is an amazing total considering he is the second most penalized player in NHL history.

Fewest penalty minutes by a 1,000-point player

210: Mike Bossy, 1977–78 to 1986–87
276: Jean Ratelle, 1960–61 to 1980–81

Bossy owns this record but the numbers really say more about Ratelle, who played 529 games more than Bossy. Ratelle scored 1,267 points in 1,281 games; Bossy 1,126 points in 752 games.

Most penalty minutes by a 1,000-game player

3,565: Dale Hunter, 1980–81 to 1999–2000

3,049: Craig Berube, 1986–87 to 2001–02*

2,972: Rick Tocchet, 1984–85 to 2001–02

(*999 games as of 2001–02)

Fewest penalty minutes by a 1,000-game player

102: Butch Goring, 1969–70 to 1984–85

117: Dave Keon, 1960–61 to 1981–82

The cleanest of the clean. Goring and Keon spent less time in the penalty box during their lengthy careers than many contemporaries would in a season or two. Goring never received a major, unlike Keon who had just one five-minute penalty for fighting.

Most penalty minutes without scoring a goal, career
370: Kim Clackson, 1979–80 to 1980–81

A defensive defenseman is a charitable way of describing this unrepentant goon, who scored just six goals in four WHA seasons. Clackson played 106 NHL games between Pittsburgh and Quebec after the renegade league folded into the NHL. In his two-year stint Clackson failed to score a single goal but racked up a record 370 penalty minutes, the most among goalless NHLers.

Most penalty minutes by a goaltender, career

584: Ron Hextall, 1986–87 to 1998–99

Until Hextall's arrival, aggressive goaltending meant boldly challenging the shooter. The Flyers netminder redefined "aggression" to include slashing, spearing and fighting.

Most penalty minutes by two brothers, career

4,991: Dale and Mark Hunter, 1980–81 to 1998–99

Who else but the hammering Hunters? Dale recorded 3,565 minutes in 1,407 games and brother Mark 1,426 minutes in 628 games.

Most seasons as penalty-minute leader
8: Red Horner, 1932–33 to 1939–40

Horner led the league in penalty minutes a record eight times, including 1933–34, when he attacked Eddie Shore after Shore blind-sided Toronto's Ace Bailey with a career-ending check. The Shore-Bailey incident remains one of hockey's darkest moments. Horner received a six-game suspension for his retaliatory actions, but earned league-wide respect. Conn Smythe later called Horner "the inspirational force behind the Leaf teams of the 1930s."

Most games by an NHL penalty leader, career

1,068: Ted Lindsay, 1944–45 to 1964–65

Bobby Hull described Lindsay as "tougher than a night in jail." One of hockey's grittiest competitors, Scarface played 17 hard-fought seasons, including 1958–59's league-leading 184-penalty-minute year.

Fewest games by an NHL penalty leader, career

ALL-TIME RECORD:

38: Joe Hall, 1917–18 to 1918–19

Hall's 38-game NHL career belies his true skill level and unfortunate demise. One of hockey's earliest bad boys, Hall enjoyed an extensive career before the NHL was formed in 1917, including winning two Stanley Cups with the Quebec Bulldogs. He became the NHL's first penalty leader and first to lead in consecutive years before his career ended tragically, a victim of an influenza epidemic during the 1919 playoffs.

MODERN-DAY RECORD:
57: Mike McMahon, 1943–44 to 1945–46
In his only full-fledged season, McMahon amassed a league-high 98 minutes and helped Montreal capture the Cup in 1943–44.

Most penalty-free seasons
5: Val Fonteyne, 1959–60 to 1971–72
Fonteyne played 13 NHL seasons without ever receiving more than two minors in a year. At best he was a fringe player and that's probably why he never won the Lady Byng Trophy for gentlemanly play. Fonteyne recorded penalty-free seasons in 1965–66, 1966–67, 1967–68, 1970–71 and 1971–72.

Most games without a penalty from start of career
83: Clint Smith, 1936–37 to 1938–39
Smith played penalty-free from his two-game NHL start in 1936–37 until February 4, 1939, a record 83 games. His first minor was his only penalty in 1938–39 and just one of his 24-minute total in 483 career games. Smith, who was an offensive threat despite his mild disposition, won the Lady Byng Trophy with the NY Rangers in 1939 and with Chicago in 1944.

Longest career without receiving a penalty
63 games: Doug Gibson, 1973–74 to 1977–78
It wasn't his lack of penalties that kept Gibson from an NHL job. He just couldn't parlay his offensive success as a junior and minor pro into the big time. His shelf-life was 63 NHL games, the longest penalty-free career in NHL annals. Curiously, long after his stints with Boston and Washington, Gibson ended his squeaky-clean

career leading Europe's VEU Feldkirch (Austria) in penalties with 137 minutes in 1983–84.

Most consecutive games without a penalty
185: Val Fonteyne, 1959–60 to 1971–72
In his 13-year career, Fonteyne took only 13 minors and never once attracted a major penalty. His longest penalty-free stretch was 185 games from February 28, 1965, to December 1, 1968.

Highest penalty minutes-per-game average (min. 2,000 PIM), career
4.72: Shane Churla, 1986–87 to 1996–97
Churla's one-dimensional play finally earned him a record: he recorded 2,301 minutes in 488 games.

Lowest penalty minutes-per-game average, career
.031: Val Fonteyne, 1959–60 to 1971–72
A Gandhi on skates, the mild-mannered Fonteyne recorded just 26 penalty minutes in 820 games.

Most penalty minutes by a 50-goal scorer, one season
254: Kevin Stevens, Pittsburgh, 1991–92
Despite spending the equivalent of about 12 games worth of ice time in the box, Stevens still set this record and scored 54 goals.
228: Keith Tkachuk, Phoenix, 1996–97
Tkachuk is big-time mean but scored a league-leading 52 goals with a .500 hockey team.

Fewest penalty minutes by a 50-goal player, one season
6: Mike Bossy, NY Islanders, 1977–78
6: Rick Kehoe, Pittsburgh, 1980–81
No two NHLers have spent less time in the box during a 50-goal

season than Kehoe and Bossy. Kehoe won the Lady Byng Trophy for his miniscule six minutes and 55 goals in 1980–81; but Bossy, the rookie sensation with 53 goals, wasn't even a consideration in 1977–78. Butch Goring won the Lady Byng that year with 37 goals and only one minor penalty.

Most penalty minutes by a 100-point player

254: Kevin Stevens, Pittsburgh, 1991–92

Stevens's 123 points in 1991–92 earned him several records. He set a single-season mark for both American-born players and left-wingers; and he was the first player in history to top 50 goals, 100 points and 200 penalty minutes in the same season.

252: Rick Tocchet, Pittsburgh, 1992–93

Cut from the same cloth as Stevens, Tocchet's career year was 1992–93, when he scored 109 points and battled for 252 penalty minutes. He was the third player in history to record 300 goals and 2,000 penalty minutes.

Fewest penalty minutes by a 100-point player

4: Jean Ratelle, NY Rangers, 1971–72

8: Mike Bossy, NY Islanders, 1983–84

8: Johnny Bucyk, Boston, 1970–71

The classy Ratelle received just two minors during his 109-point campaign of 1971–72. Bossy doubled that box time when he scored 118 points in 1983–84. Bucyk collected 116 points in 1970–71. All three won the Lady Byng Trophy as most gentlemanly player.

Most combined penalty minutes and points, one season

498: Dave Schultz, Philadelphia, 1974–75

The Hammer earned this record cooling in the box, scoring just 26 points in a record-setting 472-minute season of discontent.

Most penalty minutes by a scoring champion (min. 70 games)

154: Stan Mikita, Chicago, 1964–65, 87 points

146: Stan Mikita, Chicago, 1963–64, 89 points

143: Jean Béliveau, Montreal, 1955–56, 88 points

141: Ted Lindsay, Detroit, 1949–50, 78 points

When he broke into the NHL, Mikita was hell on wheels. He won the Art Ross Trophy with 87 points and the all-time highest penalty total among scoring leaders, a record 154 minutes.

Fewest penalty minutes by a scoring champion (min. 70 games)

12: Stan Mikita, Chicago, 1966–67, 97 points

14: Stan Mikita, Chicago, 1967–68, 87 points

16: Wayne Gretzky, Los Angeles, 1990–91, 163 points

In his own interpretation of Dr. Jekyll and Mr. Hyde, Mikita exhibited one of the game's greatest individual turnarounds to produce both the NHL's highest and lowest penalty counts by a top scorer. Within two seasons of amassing his league-record 154 minutes, the Chicago star's total dropped to just 12 minutes during his 97-point title in 1966–67. Mikita became the first player to win the Art Ross, Hart and Lady Byng trophies as top point-earner, MVP and most gentlemanly player in the same season.

Most combined points and penalty minutes by a scoring champion
299: Mario Lemieux, Pittsburgh, 1988–89
261: Wayne Gretzky, Edmonton, 1985–86

Gretzky avoided the penalty box like it was a breeding ground of contagious disease. He managed 46 minutes during his league-high 215-point season in 1985–86, but Lemieux combined 199 points and 100 minutes during 1988–89.

Most penalty minutes by a goal-scoring leader
228: Keith Tkachuk, Phoenix, 1996–97
143: Jean Béliveau, Montreal, 1955–56
125: Maurice Richard, Montreal, 1954–55

Tkachuk recorded 52 goals, Béliveau 47 goals and Richard 38 goals during their goal-leading years. Béliveau is the guy who is the surprise here.

Fewest penalty minutes by a goal-scoring leader
ALL-TIME RECORD:
4: Gordie Drillon, Toronto, 1937–38
Drillion scored 26 goals in 1937–38's 48-game schedule.

MODERN-DAY RECORD:
16: Blaine Stoughton, Hartford, 1979–80
16: Pavel Bure, Florida, 1999–2000
22: Jari Kurri, Edmonton, 1985–86
22: Brett Hull, St. Louis, 1990–91
Stoughton scored 56 goals, Bure scored 58 goals, Kurri 68 goals and Hull 86 goals in their respective seasons as top goal-scorers.

Most penalty minutes by a Norris Trophy winner
282: Chris Chelios, Chicago, 1992–93
185: Chris Chelios, Montreal, 1988–89
162: Pierre Pilote, Chicago, 1964–65
Meet Mr. Chelios, a marvellously talented rearguard with a bad attitude to match.

Fewest penalty minutes by a Norris Trophy winner

18: Red Kelly, Detroit, 1953–54

18: Nicklas Lidstrom, Detroit, 2000–01

26: Brian Leetch, NY Rangers, 1991–92

If defense means stopping your man, then doing it cleanly is an art form, and Kelly and Lidstrom are the masters.

Most combined points and penalty minutes by a Norris Trophy winner
355: Chris Chelios, Chicago, 1992–93
258: Paul Coffey, Edmonton, 1985–86
258: Chris Chelios, Montreal, 1998–89

Chelios posted a career-high 73 points in the same season he amassed a career-high 282 penalty minutes. Coffey, a player not known for his physical play, is an unexpected second. He combined 138 points and 120 penalty minutes in 1985–86.

Most penalty minutes by a Lady Byng Trophy winner

40: Frank Nighbor, Ottawa, 1925–26

40: Billy Burch, NY Americans, 1926–27

Nighbor and Burch are the first two recipients of the Lady Byng. No one has topped their 40-minute penalty total and won the award since 1926–27. One would have to surmise that the standards of cleanliness were less stringent back then.

Fewest penalty minutes by a Lady Byng Trophy winner

0: Syl Apps, Toronto, 1941–42

0: Bill Mosienko, Chicago, 1944–45

0: Bill Quackenbush, Detroit, 1948–49

Quackenbush was the first defenseman to win the most gentle-

manly player trophy and the last player so honoured with zero
penalty minutes.

Most penalty minutes by a Calder Trophy winner as top rookie

175: Denis Potvin, NY Islanders, 1973–74
141: Gary Suter, Calgary, 1985–86
Potvin established his game-play at both ends of the rink during
his rookie season, scoring 54 points and compiling a record-
setting 175-minute penalty total.

Most penalty minutes by a rookie, one season

320: Mike Peluso, Chicago, 1990–91
309: Brad May, Buffalo, 1991–92
Peluso was a one-man-wrecking crew for Chicago in his freshman year, 1990–91, posting a rookie record 320 minutes, only
30 less than NHL leader Rob Ray's 350 minutes that season.

Most penalty minutes by a goaltender, one season

113: Ron Hextall, Philadelphia, 1988–89
Hextall battled as hard as he backstopped, his wrath only
equalled by his play. He established a few NHL firsts and
was honoured many ways, but won this record without fear
or favour.

Most penalty minutes by a top-10 scorer

254: Kevin Stevens, Pittsburgh, 1991–92
211: Terry O'Reilly, Boston, 1977–78
211: Brendan Shanahan, St. Louis, 1993–94
In his devastating prime, Stevens combined that rare quality of
a banger and a sniper. He finished second overall (123 points) to
teammate Mario Lemieux in scoring while spending more time
in the box than any top-10 scorer in league history.

Largest winning margin by a penalty-minutes leader, one season

196: Dave Schultz, Philadelphia, 1974–75

No one is close to the Hammer in his record-setting season of mayhem. In a convincing impersonation of Attila the Hun, the Philly bully boy amassed 472 PIM. In second place was Moose Dupont of the Flyers with 276.

Most penalty minutes by a Hall of Famer, one season

184: Ted Lindsay, Chicago, 1958–59
175: Denis Potvin, NY Islanders, 1973–74

Lindsay, at 33 years, was one of the oldest NHL penalty leaders, racking up 184 minutes in his 15th NHL season.

Most penalty minutes in pro hockey, one season

648: Kevin Evans, IHL's Kalamazoo Wings, 1986–87

Evans's NHL career consisted of just nine games, but the five-foot nine-inch, 185-pound pit bull racked up some huge penalty numbers in the minors, most notably his 648 PIM in 73 games in Kalamazoo in 1986–87.

400-penalty-minute players, one season

PLAYER	TEAM	SEASON	PIM
Dave Schultz	Philadelphia	1974–75	472
Paul Baxter	Pittsburgh	1981–82	409
Mike Peluso	Chicago	1991–92	408
Dave Schultz	LA, Pittsburgh	1977–78	405

Highest penalty-minute total by opposing players, one game

122: Randy Holt and Frank Bathe, March 11, 1979

Randy Holt (67 minutes) and Frank Bathe (55 minutes) rank 1–2 in the NHL record books for most box time in one game. Combined they also set this mark for fisticuffs by opponents in the same game. Holt received one minor, three majors, two 10-minute misconducts and three game misconducts. Bathe earned three majors, two 10-minute misconducts and two game misconducts.

Most seasons as fighting-majors leader

4: Reggie Fleming, 1959–60 to 1970–71

Fleming established his tough-as-nails reputation during his rookie season, 1960–61, when he matched veteran fighters Lou Fontinato and Bert Olmstead with five majors. He shared the lead three more years, with four fights in 1964–65, five in 1965–66 and eight in 1967–68. Even so, these fight numbers wouldn't even rank Fleming among the NHL's top 30 pugilists today.

Most fighting majors, career

228: Craig Berube, 1986–87 to 2001–02
221: Dave "Tiger" Williams, 1974–75 to 1987–88

Berube is still about 1,000 minutes short of Williams's record as the NHL's most penalized player, but he owns this heavyweight title.

Most fighting majors, one season

39: Paul Laus, Florida, 1996–97
36: Joey Kocur, Detroit, 1985–86

When Laus hits, he hits to hurt.

Most fighting majors by a rookie, one season

37: Joey Kocur, Detroit, 1985–86

Kocur traded punches with anyone who was willing in his first full season, amassing a league-high 377 PIM in just 59 games.

Most fights, one game

5: Eddie Shore, Boston, November 23, 1929

In one mayhem-filled game, Shore fought five Maroon players: George Boucher, Dave Trottier, Hooley Smith, Red Dutton and Babe Siebert. When the dust had cleared, Trottier had suffered a lung haemorrhage, Siebert had received a broken toe, bruised ribs and a black eye, while Shore went to the hospital with a broken nose, a concussion and four missing teeth. Reports of the day say the game was delayed to scrape the blood off the ice.

Fastest fight from start of career

12 seconds: John Ferguson, Montreal, October 8, 1963

Ferguson's role in Montreal was clear from the beginning: peace-maker. Just 12 seconds into his first game he dropped the gloves with Ted Green and pummeled the Boston tough guy without mercy. Montreal had found an enforcer to keep the peace for its slick forwards.

Longest suspension for an on-ice infraction

23 games: Marty McSorley, Boston, 1999–2000
23 games: Gord Dwyer, Tampa Bay, 2000–01
21 games: Dale Hunter, Washington, 1993–94

McSorley's 23-game suspension for cracking Donald Brashear across the noggin in February 2000 was later jacked up to a full year off the ice. The tough guy, nearing the end of his career, never played another NHL game.

Longest supension for fighting with a fan
4 games: Ted Lindsay, Detroit, 1954–55

During a game at Maple Leaf Gardens on January 22, 1955, a fan named Irving Tenney reached out and grabbed Gordie Howe's stick. Howe's linemate, Ted Lindsay, attacked Tenney in retaliation, hacking him on the shoulder with his stick. The Detroit winger then dropped his stick and traded blows with Tenney. NHL president Clarence Campbell suspended Lindsay for 10 games for interfering with a spectator. After an appeal by Detroit, the sentence was reduced to four games.

Lifetime suspension for an on-ice incident
Billy Coutu, Boston, April 13, 1927

Coutu was suspended for life after assaulting referee Jerry LaFlamme and assistant Billy Bell after the last game of 1927 finals.

Lifetime suspensions for gambling
Babe Pratt, Toronto, January 29, 1946
Billy Taylor, NY Rangers, March 9, 1948
Don Gallinger, Boston, September 27, 1948

Pratt was reinstated just two weeks after his suspension for gambling. Taylor and Gallinger weren't so lucky, they had to wait until 1970.

Only player to receive a lifetime suspension and later lead the NHL in penalties
Cully Wilson, Seattle Metropolitans, 1918–19

During a February 26, 1919, game against the Victoria Aristo-crats of the Pacific Coast Hockey Association, Wilson broke

Mickey MacKay's jaw with a vicious crosscheck. Mackay was sidelined for nearly two full seasons and Wilson was eventually suspended for life from the PCHA. The next year Wilson played for the Toronto St. Pats of the NHL, where, displaying his usual aggressive style, he led the league in penalty minutes.

Only players suspended by their own general manager for excessive violence
Sprague Cleghorn and Billy Coutu, Montreal, March 7, 1923
In Game 1 of the 1923 Cup finals, Cleghorn stick-whipped Ottawa's Lionel Hitchman so severely that he had to be carted off the ice. Coutu drew a match penalty when he broke his stick over the skull of Cy Denneny after he scored the game's first goal. Montreal general manager Leo Dandurand fined the pair $200 for excessive brutality and suspended them for the next game.

Longest prison sentence by an NHL owner
5.10 years: Bruce McNall, Los Angeles, 1997
For a time in the 1990s, McNall appeared to have it all. He owned 50 racehorses, a private jet, eight homes and nine cars. But the man who brought Wayne Gretzky to California had built his empire on fraud. Ten of his 67 subsidiary companies were shams. They existed only to shuffle funds from one account to another, and most of his real companies were losing, not making money. Eventually, it all collapsed. In March 10, 1997, McNall began serving a five-year, 10-month prison sentence for swindling banks and investors out of $250 million.

CHAPTER 8

Money
doesn't talk—
it swears

According to the Fan Cost Index

compiled by TMR Inc. of Chicago, the

2001 average price for four tickets, two beers, two

soft drinks, four hot dogs, two souvenir caps,

two programs and parking for one car at an NHL

arena was $264.77. Yes, hockey has become an

expensive night out. As they say, it's a money game.

(All figures are in U.S. dollars.)

Highest team payroll, one season

$73.3 million: NY Rangers, 2001–02
$64.4 million: Detroit Red Wings, 2001–02
$61.2 million: NY Rangers, 1999–2000

It's not how much you spend, it's how well you spend. After the games-played bonus clause in Eric Lindros's salary kicked in and the acquisition of Pavel Bure in March 2002, the Broadway Blueshirts' payroll rose to a massive $73.3 million. Despite the management's fiscal largesse, the club finished a lowly 11th in the Eastern Conference. The Detroit Red Wings shelled out $64.4 million in 2001–02, finished first overall and won the Stanley Cup.

Most valuable franchise

$277 million: NY Rangers, 2001–02
$250 million: Philadelphia, 2001–02

Despite missing the playoffs for the fifth straight year, the Rangers established a new record for net worth in 2001–2002. *Forbes* magazine pegged the value of the Manhattan franchise at a hefty $277 million, proving yet again that winning has little to do with worth in the NHL.

Most millionaire players, one season

325 (approximately): 2001–02

A record destined to be surpassed.

Most million-dollar players on one team

18: NY Rangers, 2001–02

The roll call of Manhattan fat cats included Pavel Bure ($10 million), Brian Leetch ($8.7 million), Eric Lindros ($8.1 million), Theo Fleury ($6.5 million), Mike Richter ($6 million), Mark Messier ($5.6 million) and Petr Nedved

($4.2 million). Despite having more millionaires than many Fortune 500 companies, the Rangers missed the playoffs.

Most money earned by a player, one season
$28 million: Sergei Fedorov, Detroit, 1997–98
The ultimate bonus baby, Fedorov hit the free-agent jackpot when Detroit chose to match the terms of the Carolina Hurricanes' exorbitant $28-million offer sheet. In order to retain Fedorov, the Wings had to pay him a whopping $14-million signing bonus, $2 million in salary, plus a $12-million bonus as a reward for his team making the conference finals. Detroit won the Cup and Fedorov led all playoff goal-scorers.

Richest contract
$88 million: Jaromir Jagr, Washington, 2001
$87.5 million: Alexei Yashin, NY Islanders, 2001
In October 2001, Jagr cashed in by signing an eight-year $88-million deal, with the first seven years guaranteed at $77 million. Yashin joined the ranks of the filthy rich with his 10-year deal with the Isles in June 2001.

Richest contract by a concussion-prone player
$38 million: Eric Lindros, NY Rangers, 2001
After suffering six concussions, the Big E inked a four-year $38-million contract with the Rangers in 2001. The deal, which did not pay out in full unless Lindros played 50 regular-season games in 2001–02, works out to $9.5 million per annum, or about $1.6 million per concussion.

Most bang for the buck
Alexander Mogilny, Buffalo, 1992–93

Mogilny's decision to defect from the Soviet Union didn't put him in the strongest of bargaining positions in contract negotiations. Returning home was not an option unless he wanted to be sent to prison. Mogilny was earning a modest $185,000 per year when he scored a league-leading 76 goals and racked up 127 points for the Sabres in 1992–93. His salary increased to $3 million per annum the next season.

Highest salary earned, one season
$10,033,333: Jaromir Jagr, Washington, 2001–02

The Czech winger became the first NHLer to crack the $10-million barrier, surpassing the previous record-holders, Peter Forsberg, Pavel Bure and Paul Kariya, all at $10-million even.

Highest salary earned by a defenseman, one season
$9.5 million: Nicklas Lidstrom, Detroit, 2002–03
$9.5 million: Chris Pronger, St. Louis, 2001–02

Lidstrom moved atop the heap when he signed a two-year contract extension with the Wings in December 2001. The Swedish blueliner won the Norris Trophy in 2001 after being a runner-up the previous three years. Claiming the MVP award in 2000 helped boost Pronger's value. The last defenseman to win the Hart Trophy prior to Pronger was Bobby Orr in 1972. Neither Lidstrom nor Pronger are on Orr's level. It makes you wonder what No. 4 would be worth today.

Highest salary earned by a goalie, one season
$8.5 million: Patrick Roy, Colorado, 2001–02
$8 million: Dominik Hasek, Detroit, 2001–02

One might question why goalies lag behind on the NHL pay

scale. After all, they are the only players to play all 60 minutes of a game and are considered the key to playoff success, which is where the teams make big money for their owners.

Highest salary earned by a coach, one season
$1.5 million: Pat Quinn, Toronto, 2001–02
Quinn's salary included his GM duties. The three highest-paid coaches-only of all time are Scotty Bowman of Detroit, Joel Quenneville of St. Louis and Jacques Lemaire of Minnesota, all at $1.2 million.

Highest salary forfeited by a player, one season
$11 million: Peter Forsberg, Colorado, 2001–02
The gifted Swedish centre walked away from a windfall in 2001–02. Claiming his desire for the game had been eroded by health problems (he suffered a ruptured spleen in the 2001 play-offs), Forsberg took what became a season-long leave of absence, missing a chance to become hockey's highest-paid performer.

Highest salary earned in an arbitration case
$7.0 million: John LeClair, Philadelphia, 2000
$5.1 million: Bill Guerin, Boston, 2001
LeClair, whose previous contract had paid him $3.7 million annually, had asked for $9 million. The Flyers had offered $4.6 million.

Largest single-season percentage increase in salary due to arbitration
389%: Petr Sykora, New Jersey, August 2001
An NHL arbitrator awarded the 24-year-old Devils' winger a

record-setting boost in salary from $675,000 to $3.3 million. The increase was part of a two-year contract. The agreement called for Sykora to earn $3.535 million in the second year of the deal.

Most costly mistake by a general manager
$10 million: Bobby Clarke, Philadelphia, 1997–98
Clarke signed free-agent winger Chris Gratton to a five-year $16.5-million offer sheet in August 1997, of which $10 million was front-loaded to 1997–98. Gratton scored only 62 points and the Flyers made a swift exit from the playoffs. Unimpressed by his shiny new bauble, Clarke traded Gratton back to his former team, Tampa Bay, early in the 1998–99 season.

Largest bribe offered by a player
$1 billion: Ed Belfour, Dallas, 2000–01
After he was arrested in a drunken scuffle with police at a Dallas hotel in March 2000, the Stars' goalie offered police officers $100,000, then progressively upped the ante to $1 billion, if they would release him. According to arrest documents, Belfour initially wrestled with a 50-year-old hotel employee, then spit and kicked at police officers, prompting them to spray him with Mace. To cap off the evening, Belfour vomited on himself in the patrol car.

Largest fine assessed to a team
$1.5 million: St. Louis Blues, 1998
On January 4, 1999, NHL commissioner Gary Bettman imposed a record-setting fine on the Blues for a crime committed four years before: tampering with New Jersey defenseman Scott Stevens before he officially became a free agent on July 1, 1994. In addition to the monetary reparations, the Blues had to surrender two first-round draft picks to the Devils between 1999 and 2003. The next team caught tampering with a player under con-

tract to another club will pay an even harsher penalty: violation of the bylaw is now a $5-million fine.

Largest fine of an individual
$100,000: Mike Keenan, 1994

Keenan has left more burning bridges in his wake than the Luftwaffe did in World War II. After coaching the Rangers to the Cup in 1994, he deserted the club with four years remaining on his contract to sign as coach and GM of the St. Louis Blues. In the aftermath, the New York papers screamed "Rat" and "Scoundrel" and his mailbox was blown up. NHL commissioner Gary Bettman fined Keenan $100,000 and suspended him for 60 days for the "unseemly spectacle" he had created by his acrimonious departure.

Largest fine for criticizing referees

$50,000: Ed Snider, Philadelphia, May 1999

The Flyers owner racked up the heaviest fine ever levied against an individual for criticizing referees after he made disparaging comments about the officiating in his team's 1999 conference quarterfinals tilt with Toronto. Snider was incensed by an elbow penalty given to the Flyers' John LeClair by referee Terry Gregson with 2:54 left in Game 6. The Leafs scored on the resulting power play to win 1–0 and take the series. "I'm sick of this crap with the officials. I'm sick of it. It's an absolute disgrace," said Snider. Flyers coach Roger Neilson, who also ripped the officiating, was given a $25,000 fine.

Largest fine for assaulting a sportswriter

$10,000: Dominik Hasek, Buffalo, April 1997

Hasek was upset by a column written by Buffalo sportswriter

Jim Kelley that suggested the Sabres goalie lacked courage and may have been embellishing a knee injury. Before the next game, Hasek began cursing at Kelley outside the Sabres dressing room, spat on him twice and then tried to throttle the reporter with his own necktie.

Only player fined by an opposing team
Ed Belfour, Dallas, 2001–02
After he was replaced by backup goalie Marty Turco during a February 28, 2002, game in Vancouver, Belfour stormed into the dressing room and began doing some redecorating with his goalie stick. The frustrated netminder destroyed two TVs, a clock and a VCR, and smashed several holes in the walls. Canucks general manager Brian Burke later sent Belfour a bill for the damages.

Most money lost due to suspension
$335,343: Owen Nolan, San Jose, 2000–01
When high-salaried superstars get hit with a suspension, it tends to make a sizeable dent in their pocket books. Nolan was suspended for 11 games after he cold-cocked Dallas's Grant Marshall with a flying elbow on February 1, 2001. The Stars winger was removed from the ice on a stretcher. Other players have been suspended for longer periods, but no one has sacrificed more cash than Nolan.

Most expensive punch by a general manager
$20,000: George McPhee, Washington Capitals GM, 1999
When players throw 'em, they rarely have to worry about fines. But when team executives get into it, the penalties are more severe. McPhee was slapped with a $20,000 fine after he sucker-punched Blackhawks coach Lorne Molleken outside the Chicago dressing room after a penalty-filled exhibition game on Septem-

ber 25, 1999. McPhee was enraged by Chicago's bully-boy tactics in the game. Some Blackhawks players joined the altercation, tearing McPhee's suit and bloodying his face before security guards quelled the melee.

Most money lost to injury
$9.5 million: Montreal, 1999–2000

The Canadiens lost a record 536 man-games to injury in 1999–2000, which amounted to nearly $10 million of their $32-million player budget. Only one regular, Patrick Poulin, played all 82 games. Not surprisingly, Montreal missed the playoffs.

Largest disability insurance settlement paid back by a player
$6 million: Bryan Berard, NY Rangers, 2001–02

Berard retired after suffering severe damage to his right eye when he was hit by a stick during a game in March 2000. The former Toronto defenseman underwent seven eye surgeries and had special contact lenses inserted to improve his vision and then mounted a comeback with the Rangers. In order to return to the NHL, Berard had to pay back $6 million on his insurance settlement.

Most money collected by a player in the 1996 lawsuit between retired players and the NHL
$205,005: Gordie Howe

After a five-year court battle, the Supreme Court of Canada ruled that 1,343 players would receive lump-sum payments for misappropriated pension money collected by the NHL between 1947 and 1982. Based on age, years of service and pension contributions, Howe received the highest amount.

Most money lost by a player in a contract dispute
$3.6 million: Alexei Yashin, Ottawa, 1999–2000

On the advice of his agent Mark Gandler, Yashin refused to
report to the Senators and honour the last year of his contract
in 1999–2000. Ottawa refused to knuckle under and trade the
recalcitrant Russian, who sat out the entire season. An inde-
pendent arbitrator later ruled that Yashin still legally owed
Ottawa a year on his contract. He played for Ottawa in 2000–01
at $3.6 million, thus sacrificing even more cash that he could
have been earning on a new contract.

Most money deferred by players to allow their team to sign another player
$1.5 million: Steve Yzerman, Brendan Shanahan, Chris Chelios, Detroit, 2001–02

In a hockey first, the three Detroit veterans agreed to each
defer about $500,000 of their salaries to free up the funds
the club needed to sign free-agent Brett Hull to a two-year
$9.5-million deal.

Most money spent by a team on free agents, one summer
$115 million: Colorado Avalanche, 2001

The Avalanche doled out a stunning $115 million to re-sign three
stars from its Cup-winning squad: Joe Sakic ($9.8 million), Rob
Blake ($9.3 million) and Patrick Roy ($8.5 million). The trio
earned more than $27 million in 2001–02, more than entire
player payrolls of seven NHL teams.

CHAPTER 9

The firing
line

The only listed NHL record for shots
on goal is Phil Esposito's 550-shot
count from 1970–71. Paul Kariya ranks second with
429 in 1998–99. But who holds the all-time career
mark? Or the rookie record? Or the most shots
without scoring? All credible records worthy of . . .
well . . . a record. (Shots on goals statistics are only
available from 1967–68.)

Most shots on goal, career

6,206: Ray Bourque, 1979–80 to 2001–01

In 22 seasons and 1,612 games, Bourque never averaged less than 200 shots per year except 1979–80 (185 shots).

Most shots on goal by a forward, career

5,089: Wayne Gretzky 1979–80 to 1998–99

Gretzky's scored his record 894 goals on 5,089 shots; a shooting percentage of 17.6 per cent.

Most shots on goal by a defenseman, one season
413: Bobby Orr, Boston, 1969–70
392: Bobby Orr, Boston, 1970–71
390: Ray Bourque, Boston, 1995–96

Orr's breakout year was 1969–70, when he scored 33 goals and 120 points to produce the first scoring title by a defenseman. It was also the year Orr established his rearguard record 413 shots. Only three players have stockpiled more blasts in the regular-season: Phil Esposito, Paul Kariya and Bobby Hull.

Fewest shots on goal by a Norris Trophy winner

126: Rod Langway, Washington, 1982–83

133: Larry Robinson, Montreal, 1979–80

In his first season with Washington, Langway set the tone for his 11-year reign as leader of the Caps. He wasn't there to blast rubber but rather to shore up the defense. Under his watch, the Caps moved from the cellar to respectability, allowing 55 fewer goals and improving by 29 points. Langway's 126 shots in 1979–80 was 287 less than Bobby Orr's record of 413 by Norris Trophy winners.

Fewest shots on goal by a scoring champion (min. 70 games)

187: Bryan Trottier, NY Islanders, 1978–79
212: Wayne Gretzky, Los Angeles, 1990–91

Compared to Phil Esposito's record 550 shots by a scoring leader, Trottier was practically playing stay-at-home defense when he blasted an all-time low 187 shots to win the Art Ross Trophy in 1978–79. More impressive is his 25.1 shooting percentage, scoring consistently a goal on every four shots on net. Trottier was also well below the average shot count taken by scoring champions to win the title: 322 shots.

Fewest shots on goal by a goal-scoring leader (min. 70 games)

213: Charlie Simmer, Los Angeles, 1979–80, 56 goals
234: Blaine Stoughton, Hartford, 1979–80, 56 goals
236: Jari Kurri, Edmonton, 1985–86, 68 goals

Simmer's role on the Kings' Triple Crown Line was to put the puck in the net, which the left-winger did with deadly efficiency. Stoughton performed the same task for Hartford. Kurri was Wayne Gretzky's triggerman on the Oilers.

Fewest shots on goal by a 50-goal scorer

171: Charlie Simmer, Los Angeles, 1980–81, 56 goals
177: Craig Simpson, Pittsburgh/Edmonton, 1987–88, 56 goals
186: Hakan Loob, Calgary, 1987–88, 50 goals
186: Gary Roberts, Calgary, 1991–92, 53 goals

Simmer could have moonlighted as a professional hit man. At six foot three and 210 pounds, he may have had the softest hands of any big forward in NHL history. Simmer lit the lamp on 32.7 per cent of his shots in 1980-81, a record for a 50-goal man.

Most shots on goal by a rookie, one season

387: Teemu Selanne, Winnipeg, 1992–93

Selanne's rookie year of 76 goals and 132 points obliterated the rookie marks of some great freshmen (Mike Bossy and Peter Stastny) but he would never have amassed such totals without his "other" rookie record: 387 shots on net.

Most consecutive goal-scoring shots from start of career

4: Jan Caloun, San Jose, 1995–96

Caloun's NHL debut was a marvel. He scored on each of his first four shots in his first three games from March 18 to March 22, 1996. The Czech winger concluded his 11-game rookie season with eight goals on 20 shots, an accuracy rate of 40 per cent.

Most shots on goal without scoring a goal, one season

153: Gilles Marotte, Chicago, 1967–68

Marotte iced a lot of blueline time but couldn't bulge the twine once in 153 shots during 1967–68. His aim improved over his 12-year career, but never better than 1971–72's 10 goals on 203 shots, a shooting percentage of just 4.9 per cent.

Most shots on goal, one game

19: Ray Bourque, Boston, March 21, 1991
19: Gordie Howe, Detroit, January 27, 1955

Bourque holds this unofficial mark, but according to some sources (with shot totals prior to 1967), Howe shares the lead with his own 19-shot effort in 1954–55. Interestingly, both matches ended in 3–3 ties but Bourque scored a goal on his 14th shot while Howe, for all his work, went scoreless. Howe did, however, outshoot the entire New York team, which fired just 18 shots that night compared to Detroit's 31. In their game, Boston fired a modern-day record 73 shots on Quebec; the Bruins handled just 26 shots.

CHAPTER 10

Welcome
to the
shooting gallery

Gump Worsley once claimed that the only job worse than being a goalie was a javelin catcher at a track meet. His all-star wit aside, the Gumper was one of the most shell-shocked netminders to brave the NHL's six-team era, a time when guarding the goal was a far more perilous profession without bullet-proof masks and high-tech protective equipment.

Most shots faced, career

26,630: Patrick Roy, 1984–85 to 2001–02

24,708: John Vanbiesbrouck 1981–82 to 2001–02

Most shots faced, one season (since 1954–55)

2,438: Felix Potvin, Toronto, 1996–97

2,382: Curtis Joseph, St. Louis, 1993–94

The hail of rubber that Potvin faced during 1996–97 with an inept Leafs team would affect most goalies' nerves and confidence. It may have adversely affected his. It took him several years to regain his form after this onslaught. The Cat faced an average of 34.3 shots per game. The Leafs replaced Potvin with Joseph, another goalie accustomed to nightly shelling.

Most shots faced, one game

83: Sam LoPresti, Chicago, March 4, 1941

LoPresti, a rookie from Eveleth, Minnesota, stepped into a shooting gallery at Boston Garden and despite his record 80 shots stopped he still came out a loser in the 3–2 defeat against first-place Boston. Ironically, his goaltending opponent that night, Frank Brimsek, was also from Eveleth. Later, when asked whether LoPresti had been good or lucky, Boston defenseman Johnny Crawford stated: "He was good alright. If he hadn't been good he wouldn't be alive now."

Most shots faced by a goalie who did not lose, one game

73: Ron Tugnutt, Quebec, March 21, 1991

Boston Garden was also the scene of this blast zone. The shell-shocked Tugnutt made 70 saves in 60 minutes to preserve a 3–3 tie for the overwhelmed Nordiques. Boston defenseman Ray Bourque fired 19 shots on net by himself.

Most combined shots faced by opposing goalies, one game

141: Roy Worters, Pittsburgh Pirates, against Jake Forbes, NY Americans, December 26, 1925

Was there a super-sale on rubber? Worters faced 73 shots and Forbes, 68 in this Boxing Day shootout. The Americans won 3–1.

Highest shots-per-game average, one season (min. 30 games, since 1954–55)

38.3: Ron Low, Washington, 1974–75, in 48 games
38.2: Gump Worsley, NY Rangers, 1962–63, in 67 games

Tending goal for the expansion Capitals was an exercise in masochism. Low was assaulted nightly with more than three dozen shots, many of them unstoppable. It's hard to imagine that he slept soundly that season. Worsley's brilliance with the Rangers is underscored by this amazing figure from hockey's Golden Age. Despite the torrent of frozen disks fired his way he managed to post a respectable 3.27 GAA. The next season, Worsley was mercifully traded to Montreal, saving his career and his sanity.

Highest save percentage, one season (min. 40 games)

.942: Jacques Plante, Toronto, 1970–71
.937: Dominik Hasek, Buffalo, 1998–99

Jake the Snake's play for a mediocre Leafs team, at age 42, was extraordinary. His impact can be gauged by examining Toronto's record. The Leafs were 24–11–4 with Plante in the nets, and 13–22–4 without him. Based on his 64-game work load, Hasek, who ranks second with a .937 save percentage in 1998–99, may have turned in the most impressive season of all time. Hasek logged 24 more games and faced 612 more shots than Plante did in 1970–71.

Most wins, career (incl. playoffs)

664: Patrick Roy, 1984–85 to 2001–02
506: Jacques Plante, 1952–53 to 1972–73
500: Terry Sawchuk, 1949–50 to 1969–70

The same netminder who leads in all-time regular-season
wins leads in combined wins. Roy has 516 regular-season and
148 playoff wins and counting.

Most regular-season wins by a goalie who did not win the Stanley Cup, career

374: John Vanbiesbrouck, 1981–82 to 2001–02

The Beezer's only real crack at the Cup came in 1996, when he
backstopped the upstart Florida Panthers to the finals. Colorado
spanked the Cats in four straight.

Most consecutive winning seasons (20 wins or more)

9: Jacques Plante, Montreal, 1954–55 to 1962–63
9: Patrick Roy, Montreal, 1985–86 to 1993–94

Plante's streak ended when he was traded to the NY Rangers
in 1963–64. That season he lost 36 games, double his highest
single-season loss total with Montreal. Roy's streak ended
when Montreal crumbled during the lockout-shortened
1994–95 season.

Longest gap between regular-season wins
10 years: Ben Grant, 1933–34 to 1943–44

After playing 29 NHL games over five seasons, Grant was demoted to
the minors in 1933–34, and had actually been retired for a year
before Toronto signed him as a free-agent replacement for Turk Broda
in 1943–44.

Longest gap between first and second wins

10 years: Bob Champoux, 1964 playoffs to 1973–74

Champoux, a 21-year-old rookie, was pressed into service as a replacement for injured Terry Sawchuk in Game 2 of the Wings 1964 semifinals series against Bobby Hull and his Chicago shooters. Detroit won 5–4. Champoux didn't play another game in the NHL until 1973–74 with the Golden Seals, when he posted the only two regular-season victories of his career.

Best winning percentage, career (230 wins or more)

.758: Ken Dryden, Montreal, 1970–71 to 1978–79

.658: Gerry Cheevers, Boston, 1961–62 to 1979–80

Good as Dryden was, we can't forget that he played for one of hockey's most powerful dynasties. In 397 games he netted an unbelievable 258–57–74 record. Cheevers had a 230–102–74 career in 418 games.

Most wins, one season (incl. playoffs)

59: Bernie Parent, Philadelphia, 1973–74

59: Martin Brodeur, New Jersey, 1999–2000

58: Mike Richter, NY Rangers, 1993–94

Parent holds the NHL record with 47 regular-season wins, but combined with playoff totals, he has to share the all-time lead with Brodeur. Both netminders won the Stanley Cup in their respective years but the longer postseason in 2000 earned Brodeur 16 wins compared to Parent's 12 wins. Richter recorded a combined 42 regular-season and 16 playoff wins.

Most wins by a rookie, one season

44: Terry Sawchuk, Detroit, 1950–51

43: Ed Belfour, Chicago, 1990–91

Both these keepers won the Calder Trophy. Sawchuk's flashy

arrival spelled the end of Harry Lumley's career in the Motor City. Belfour hit the big time with a bang straight out of Saginaw of the IHL.

Most wins for an expansion team, one season

22: Lorne Chabot, NY Rangers, 1926–27

22: Ron Tugnutt, Columbus, 2000–01

Fortified with stars from the defunct Western Canadian Hockey League, the Rangers weren't an expansion club in the modern-day sense. The beetle-browed Chabot (22–9–5) led them to first place in the NHL's American Division during 1926–27. Tugnutt did more with less, posting a 2.44 GAA and a 22–25–5 record for the talent-starved Blue Jackets.

Most wins in their only NHL season

10: Harvey Bennett, Boston 1944–45

10: Hec Highton, Chicago, 1943–44

10: Herb Rheaume, Montreal, 1925–26

Bennett and Highton were both World War II call-ups. Bennett earned a 10–12–2 record; Highton had 10–14–0 in his lone season. Rheaume was a stop-gap between Montreal greats Georges Vezina, who was felled by tuberculosis, and George Hainsworth.

Best winning percentage, one season (min. 40 games)

.875: Tiny Thompson, Boston, 1929–30

.830: Bill Durnan, Montreal, 1943–44

.830: Chris Osgood, Detroit, 1995–96

In just his second season with the Bruins, Thompson established himself as the league's best goalie with a 38–5–1 record. Durnan posted a 38–5–7 mark. Osgood was 39–6–5.

Longest winning streak, one season

17: Gilles Gilbert, Boston, 1975–76

Despite setting this record and posting an impressive 33–8–10 record in 1975–76, Gilbert had trouble making a believer out of coach Don Cherry. He lost the starter's role soon after to Gerry Cheevers, who had returned from the WHA.

Longest undefeated streak, one season

32 games: Gerry Cheevers, Boston, 1971–72
31 games: Pete Peeters, Boston, 1982–83

Cheevers was never a GAA leader, but few other puck stoppers were better at winning. Peeters came close to matching Cheevers's record a decade later with a less dominant Boston team. Cheevers delivered a 24–0–8 record; Peeters, 26–0–5.

Longest undefeated streak by a rookie, one season

27 games: Pete Peeters, Philadelphia, 1979–80

Peeters (22–0–5) clearly benefited from being a part of a Flyers team that played a record 35 straight games without a loss. Even so, he had a 31-game undefeated streak with the Bruins too.

Longest undefeated streak from start of a career

16 games: Patrick Lalime, Pittsburgh, 1996–97

Lalime may have raised the Penguins' expectations too high with his sizzling 14–0–2 start. He went 7–12 the rest of his rookie season before his rights were traded to Anaheim for Sean Pronger in 1998. It was not the brightest of decisions.

Most losses, career

352: Gump Worsley, 1952–53 to 1973–74
351: Gilles Meloche, 1970–71 to 1987–88

A one-loss difference. Did Meloche know when to quit, sparing him the humility of owning this record? He stopped at 788 games, while Worsley played in 861 contests, including 10 miserable seasons with a pathetic Rangers team. Meloche spent seven seasons getting kicked around with the Golden Seals and the Barons.

Most losses, one season
48: Gary Smith, California, 1970–71
47: Al Rollins, Chicago, 1953–54

Smith (19–48–4) and Rollins (12–47–7) were both first-rate goalies who shared the misfortune of playing for terrible teams. In fact, despite losing more games than any goalkeeper in history to that point, Rollins won the Hart Trophy as MVP with the last-place Hawks in 1953–54.

Fewest losses, one season, (min. 50 games)
5: Bill Durnan, Montreal, 1943–44
6: Ken Dryden, Montreal, 1976–77
6: Mike Vernon, Calgary, 1988–89
6: Chris Osgood, Detroit, 1995–96

Durnan was a rookie. Unlike the others listed here, he played in every one of his team's games and posted a 38–5–7 record. Dryden was 41–6–8; Vernon, 37–6–5; and Osgood, 39–6–5.

Fewest losses, one season, (min. 60 games)
8: Ken Dryden, Montreal, 1971–72
10: Ken Dryden, Montreal, 1975–76

Dryden never lost more than 10 games in his eight-year career, recording personal bests of 39–8–15 in 1971–72 and 42–10–8 in 1975–76.

Fewest losses, one season, (min. 70 games)

13: Bernie Parent, Philadelphia, 1973–74

13: Terry Sawchuk, Detroit, 1950–51

Parent's goaltending was the key to the Broad Street Bullies' success. It was only because he was such a wall in the net that they could afford to take so many penalties. Parent had a 47–13–12 year; Sawchuk was 44–13–13.

Best goals-against average, career

ALL-TIME RECORD

1.91: Alex Connell, 1924–25 to 1936–37

1.93: George Hainsworth, 1926–27 to 1936–37

Known as "The Ottawa Fireman" because he worked part-time for the fire department, Connell extinguished a lot of flames on the ice too. Despite owning this record, he only led the league in GAA once in his 12-year career.

MODERN DAY-RECORD

2.21: Martin Brodeur, 1991–92 to 2001–02

2.23: Dominik Hasek, 1990–91 to 2001–02

2.24: Ken Dryden, Montreal, 1970–71 to 1978–79

Brodeur and Hasek's sterling numbers indicate how much scoring declined in Gary Bettman's NHL.

Worst goals-against average, career (min. 200 games)

4.28: Ron Low, 1972–73 to 1984–85

4.27: John Garrett, 1979–80 to 1984–85

4.24: Michel Dion, 1979–80 to 1984–85

All these puck stoppers owed their jobs to expansion. Low had the handicap of toiling three seasons with the lowly Washington Capitals and having his career overlap with hockey's highest-scoring era.

Most years leading in goals-against average

9: Jacques Plante, Montreal (7), St. Louis (1), Toronto (1),
   1952–53 to 1972–73
7: Clint Benedict, Ottawa (6), Montreal Maroons (1),
   1917–18 to 1929–30

Best goals-against average, one season (min. 40 games)

ALL-TIME RECORD

0.92: George Hainsworth, Montreal, 1928–29

Hainsworth set this stunning mark during a season in which the
NHL's highest-scoring team averaged just two goals per game.

MODERN-DAY RECORD

1.77: Al Rollins, Toronto, 1950–51
1.77: Tony Esposito, Chicago, 1971–72
1.79: Ron Tugnutt, Ottawa, 1998–99

Worst goals-against average, one season (min. 30 games)

6.24: Ken McAuley, NY Rangers, 1943–44

Nicknamed "Tubby," the Edmonton-born McAuley was another
wartime replacement goalie. The Rangers gave Tubby little support.
After absorbing a 15–0 pasting by the Red Wings on January 23,
1944, New York didn't win another game the rest of the season.

Largest winning margin in goals-against average, one season

0.82: Bill Durnan, Montreal, 1943–44
0.80: Bill Durnan, Montreal, Montreal, 1944–45

Durnan had a 2.18 GAA in 1943–44. Runner-up, Paul Bibeault of
Toronto, was at 3.00. Durnan was one of the few legitimate big-
league goalies in the NHL during the war years.

Only goalie to lead in goals-against average with a non-playoff team

Roy Worters: NY Americans, 1930–31

There are few more unusual entries in the record book than Worters's league-best 1.61 GAA in 1930–31. Goalies with the best GAA nearly always come from the ranks of the elite teams, but the Americans finished seventh in a 10-team NHL circuit.

Worst goals-against average by a goalie who played only one game

15.00: Jim Stewart, Boston, January 10, 1980

Stewart, a Cambridge, Massachusetts, native, gave up five goals in the first 20 minutes of his NHL debut against the Rangers and then got the hook. That was his only taste of big-league action.

Most goals allowed, career

2,756: Gilles Meloche, 1970–71 to 1987–88
2,756, Grant Fuhr, 1981–82 to 1999–2000

Bizarre, but true. Meloche and Fuhr are tied for the lead in this category. Meloche played in 788 games; Fuhr in 868 games.

Most goals allowed, one season

310: Ken McAuley, NY Rangers, 1943–44
282: Greg Millen, Hartford, 1982–83
258: Greg Millen, Pittsburgh, 1980–81

GM Lester Patrick knew his Rangers were going to tank (he tried to suspend operations during World War Two), he just didn't know how low they could go. His goalie, McAuley, was bombed worse than any European city in the war. Millen may not have been as bad as the numbers suggest. But Pittsburgh and Hartford were.

Most goals allowed, one game

16: Frank Brophy, Quebec Bulldogs, March 3, 1920

15: Ken McAuley, NY Rangers, January 23, 1944

15: Doug Soetaert, Winnipeg, November 11, 1981

A bad night for Brophy, losing 16–3 to Montreal, but then he had quite a few that season. The 19-year-old Brophy logged a horrendous 7.11 GAA in 21 games with the last-place Bulldogs. McAuley suffered through his own double-digit nightmare, a 15–0 defeat to Detroit. In the age of tandem goalies, what were the Jets thinking, leaving Soetaert to swing in the wind and handle all 51 shots in their 15–2 wipe-out against Minnesota?

Most goals allowed by a goalie tandem, one game

14: Michel Larocque and Jiri Crha, Toronto, March 19, 1981

Buffalo embarrassed Toronto 14–4 as Larocque gave up 10 goals (a record nine goals in the second period alone) and Crha allowed the other four in the third frame.

Most goals allowed by different goalies during one power play

3: Red Horner, King Clancy and Alex Levinsky, Toronto, March 15, 1932

Three different substitute Leaf players—Red Horner, King Clancy and Alex Levinsky—all took a turn in net and were scored upon in a two-minute penalty to Toronto goalie Lorne Chabot. Old-time netminders served their own infractions in the penalty box. Although it was the rule of the day, not many managers liked it. As referee Bill Stewart was following a play down the ice, Leaf manager Conn Smythe reached out from the bench and grabbed him by the sweater. Stewart ordered him evicted from the game. Smythe refused to leave, creating a small riot between players and Boston Garden officials. Boston beat Toronto 6–2.

Most goals allowed by a goalie who played only one NHL game
10: Ron Loustel, Winnipeg, March 27, 1981
"There's no place like home" is not an expression the Winnipeg-born Loustel can relate to, considering the humiliating experience he faced before a hometown crowd for his only NHL game. Vancouver waltzed to a 10–2 victory.

Fastest hat trick allowed
21 seconds: Lorne Anderson, NY Rangers, March 23, 1952
Anderson was the victim of Bill Mosienko's famous hat trick. The Chicago winger scored at 6:09, 6:20 and 6:30 of the third period in a 7–6 Hawks win. It was the final game of the 1951–52 season. Anderson, a rookie from Renfrew, Ontario, played in only three NHL games and this was his swan song.

Most five-goal games allowed, one season
3: Howard Lockhart, Hamilton Tigers, 1920–21
Lockhart's nickname was Holes, a fitting moniker considering his play in 1920–21. He surrendered five goals to Montreal's Newsy Lalonde in a 10–5 pasting on February 16, 1921; six goals to Corb Denney of the Toronto St. Pats in a 10–3 drubbing on January 26, 1921; and another six to Cy Denneny of the Ottawa Senators in a 12–5 landslide on March 7, 1921.

Most 50th goals allowed, career
6: Denis Herron, 1972–1973 to 1985–86
Herron allowed three 50th goals by Guy Lafleur and one each by Michel Goulet, Tim Kerr and Wayne Gretzky.

Most 50th goals allowed, one season

3: Tom Barrasso, Pittsburgh, 1987–88

Barrasso gave up 50th goals by Steve Yzerman, Joe Nieuwendyk and Stephane Richer.

Most shutouts for one team, career

85: Terry Sawchuk, Detroit, 1949–50 to 1969–70

75: George Hainsworth, Montreal, 1926–27 to 1936–37

Hockey's shutout king recorded 83 per cent of his all-time record 103 shutouts in Motown.

Most shutouts by one-team goalie, career

62: Turk Broda, Toronto, 1936–37 to 1951–52

55: Martin Brodeur, New Jersey, 1991–92 to 2001–02

The man they called Turkey Eyes played for five Cup winners in Toronto.

Most shutout titles

7: Clint Benedict, Ottawa, 1917–18 to 1929–30

6: Glenn Hall, Detroit, Chicago, St, Louis, 1952–53 to 1970–71

Benedict won seven shutout titles with the Senators from 1917–18 to 1923–24. His highest total of shutouts in any of those years was five, an indication of the wide-open play during the NHL's first few seasons.

Most shutouts, one season

ALL-TIME RECORD:

22: George Hainsworth, Montreal, 1928–29

Hainsworth recorded zeroes in 50 per cent of the Canadiens'

games. Oddly, the Habs posted wins in only 16 of his shutouts. Six of his goose eggs were scoreless draws.

15: Tony Esposito, Chicago, 1969–70

Esposito earned his nickname Tony O with this startling freshman performance for the Blackhawks.

Most shutouts by a rookie, one season

15: Tony Esposito, Chicago, 1969–70
12: Tiny Thompson, Boston, 1926–27

Esposito played 63 games; Thompson, 44 games. Still, despite the sizeable games-played difference, it's remarkable that a modern-day netminder topped an old guy.

Most shutouts by a goalie in last NHL season

15: Hal Winkler, Boston, 1927–28

Despite the 15 zeroes, Winkler's NHL career ended at age 36, when he was replaced in the Beantown cage by 22-year-old rookie Tiny Thompson.

Only goalie to record more shutouts than wins, one season
Joe Miller, Pittsburgh Pirates, 1928–29

Given the 44-game schedule of 1928–29, Miller's 11 shutouts look impressive. But before forward passing rules were instituted, netminders were king and zeroes plentiful. Six of the 11 zeros by Miller were scoreless ties; and he had 14 shutouts against him. Miller logged just nine wins and a 1.73 GAA for the punchless Pirates.

Longest shutout sequence

461 minutes, 29 seconds: Alex Connell, Ottawa, 1927–28

Connell recorded six straight shutouts, three of them in scoreless ties, before Chicago's Duke Keats finally put a puck past
him in the second period of the seventh game.

Most shutouts, one month

6: George Hainsworth, Montreal, January 1929
6: George Hainsworth, Montreal, February 1929
6: Dominik Hasek, Buffalo, December 1997

Another amazing feat by a modern goalie. Until Hasek's
dazzling December in 1997, Hainsworth's record had stood
for 68 years.

Most teams with recorded shutouts, career

6: Lorne Chabot, 1926–27 to 1936–37
6: Sean Burke, 1987–88 to 2001–02

It's anyone's guess why these two were traded so often.

Most seasons

21: Terry Sawchuk, 1949–50 to 1969–70
21: Gump Worsley, 1952–53 to 1973–74

This is a long time to see service in the nets. It's even more
remarkable when you consider the physical toll exacted on
goalies during Sawchuk and Worsley's era. In those days,
padding being what it was, every hard shot left a bruise.

Most seasons with one team

14: Turk Broda, Toronto, 1936–37 to 1951–52
14: Mike Richter, NY Rangers, 1988–89 to 2001–02

Broda fit like a glove with Toronto, a team that was at the height
of its glory when he was backstopping them.

Most consecutive complete games, career

502: Glenn Hall, 1955–56 to 1962–63

Beset by bad nerves, Hall tossed his cookies before every game. He once said, "Playing goal is a winter of torture for me." His streak lasted from October 6, 1955, to November 7, 1962.

Most consecutive complete games, (incl. playoffs)
551: Glenn Hall, 1955–56 to 1962–63

Hockey's most unbreakable record. During Hall's 502-game streak, he played another 49 playoff games before finally sitting out his first game in seven years in November 1962.

Most games with one team, career

873: Tony Esposito, Chicago, 1969–70 to 1983–84

Aside from 13 games in his first season with Montreal, Esposito played his entire career in Chicago.

Most games by a one-team goalie, career

653: Mike Richter, NY Rangers, 1988–89 to 2001–02
629: Turk Broda, Toronto, 1936–37 to 1951–52

It takes a special athlete to make it in New York. Richter's run on Broadway is a show-stopping feat.

Most games without a start, career

12: Bruce Racine, St. Louis, 1995–96

Racine was hockey's version of a baseball relief pitcher. In 1995–96, he came on as a substitute in 11 regular-season games and one in the playoffs for the Blues. Coach Mike Keenan used Racine to give first-stringer Grant Fuhr the occasional breather.

Most games without a shutout, career

132: Pokey Reddick, 1986–87 to 1993–94

Reddick may not be proud of this record, but then a lot of goalies can't claim more than a hundred games in the big show.

Most consecutive games allowing two goals or less

18: Jacques Plante, Montreal, 1959–60

This record was long overshadowed by another goaltending feat of far more significance. Seven games into his 15–0–3 record between October 22 and December 3, 1959, Plante became the first netminder to regularly wear a mask. The date was November 1. In the subsequent 11 games, Plante was scored upon just 13 times.

Most games without a playoff appearance, career

287: Dunc Wilson, 1969–70 to 1978–79

Few goalies had Wilson's knack or timing for playing on teams during their lean years. He bounced from Philadelphia to Vancouver, Toronto, NY Rangers and Pittsburgh. The upside? Wilson got an early start on his golf game each spring.

Longest gap between NHL appearances

18 years: Moe Roberts, from 1933–34 to 1951–52

Roberts played what everyone thought was his last NHL game in December 1933 with the NY Americans. But 19 years later, Roberts, who was employed as Chicago's assistant trainer, filled in for injured starter Harry Lumley against Detroit on November 25, 1951. The 45-year-old played the final period and did not allow a goal.

Most games, one season (incl. playoffs)

97: Martin Brodeur, New Jersey, 2000–01
95: Martin Brodeur, New Jersey, 1999–2000

Brodeur has never received the attention he deserves for his yeoman work ethic. In a two-year span he played 192 games, or about three seasons of action for first-string NHL goalies. Grant Fuhr holds the regular-season record with 79 games, in 1995–96.

Most games by a rookie, one season
74: Ed Belfour, Chicago, 1990–91
Belfour's coach that year was Mike Keenan, who believes in playing his stars until they drop.

Most games in final season
70: Frank Brimsek, Chicago, 1949–50
Out of a possible 542 games during his 10-year career, Brimsek played in 514, including six complete seasons. In his last four campaigns he missed only six games.

Most minutes, career
57,254: Terry Sawchuk, 1949–50 to 1969–70
In human time, that's about 40 days and nights.

Fewest minutes, career
3: Robbie Irons, St. Louis, November 13, 1968
3: Christian Soucy, Chicago, March 31, 1994
Irons's brief big-league stint came when Blues' starter Glenn Hall was tossed out of a game against the Rangers for disputing a goal by Vic Hadfield. Coach Scotty Bowman had Jacques Plante quickly suit up and replace Irons after three uneventful minutes. Soucy replaced Chicago starter Jeff Hackett for the last three minutes of a game against Washington.

Most minutes in goal by a position player, career

192: Harry Mummery, 1919–20 and 1921–22

Mummery, a defenseman, made four appearances in goal, three with the Quebec Bulldogs in 1919–20, and one with the Hamilton Tigers in 1921–22. He gave up 20 goals in his 192 minutes in the barrel.

Most goals, career

2: Ron Hextall, Philadelphia, 1986–87 to 1998–99
2: Martin Brodeur, New Jersey, 1991–92 to 2001–02

Hextall hit the bulls-eye against the Boston Bruins on December 8, 1987, after Boston yanked its goalie for an extra attacker. Hextall was also the first masked man to score a playoff goal, hitting the empty net against the Washington Captals in an 8–5 Flyers win in the 1989 division semifinals. Brodeur scored his pair against Montreal in the first round of the 1997 playoffs and in February 2000 against Philadelphia.

Only goalie to score on an opposing goalie

Fred Brophy, CAHL Westmount, ECAHA Montreal, 1905 and 1906

Goalies are a proud bunch. Embarrass them and they'll make damn sure to get even. In Brophy's case, the target was occasionally his own players, who, during really bad games, were served up a little humble pie by their netminder with his coast-to-coast rushes. On February 18, 1905, the game out of hand, Brophy dashed across the rink and potted one against Quebec goalie Paddy Moran. Brophy's Westmount team lost 17–5. Just to prove it wasn't the exception, on March 7, 1906, against the Montreal Victorias, Brophy scored on goalkeeper Nathan Frye after another end-to-end rush, eluding such old-timers as Russell Bowie and Joe Eveleigh. Brophy's team was whipped 14–6 in that contest. These two goals by a goalie (on a team in a league competing for the Stanley Cup) stood until Billy Smith was credited with the NHL's first goal by a goaltender in 1979.

Only goalie to score a game-winning goal
Martin Brodeur, New Jersey, February 15, 2000
Brodeur got his milestone marker in the third period of a game against Philadelphia. He was the last Devils player to touch a puck that Flyers forward Daymond Langkow accidentally directed into his own net with goalie Brian Boucher on the bench during a delayed penalty. The fluke goal stood up as the winner in New Jersey's 4–2 victory.

Only goalie to score a power-play goal
Evgeni Nabokov, San Jose, March 10, 2002
How does something like this happen? In this case, it was because Canucks coach Marc Crawford opted to pull goalie Peter Skudra in the last minute with his team trailing 6–4, even though Canucks winger Jarko Ruutu was serving a major penalty. At the 19:12 mark, Nabokov corralled the loose puck and deftly flipped it the length of the ice into the empty cage.

Most points, career
48: Tom Barrasso, 1983–84 to 2001–02
46: Grant Fuhr, 1981–82 to 1999–2000
Barrasso earned all points on assists, which presents an even more interesting record: most career points by a player without a goal.

Most points, one season

14: Grant Fuhr, Edmonton, 1983–84

9: Curtis Joseph, St. Louis, 1991–92

Aided by the quick-strike capability of his Oiler teammates, Fuhr recorded a single-season goalie record of 14 assists in 1983–84, despite appearing in only 45 games. Incredibly, Fuhr outscored 62 other NHL skaters who played as many or more games that season.

Most points, one game

3: Jeff Reese, Calgary, February 10, 1993

Reese, the only netminder ever nicknamed Pieces, tallied a record three assists in Calgary's 13–1 demolition of the San Jose Sharks.

Most vomiting episodes, career
1,021: Glenn Hall, 1951–52 to 1970–71

Hall probably had the strongest stomach muscles of any goalie. The nerve-racked goalie exercised them before each game by retching into a bucket. Hall once explained that he didn't fear playing goal. What he feared was not playing well.

Most leeches used, one season

2: Ed Johnston, Boston, 1963–64

Johnston, who did not wear a mask, was made of stern stuff. In 1963–64, he became the last NHL netminder to play every minute of the schedule. He suffered four broken noses with the last-place Boston Bruins in that 70-game season. On two occasions, his eyes were so swollen that doctors had to apply leeches to his face to suck up the blood so he could see well enough to don his gear. But play he did, all 4,200 painful minutes.

Most bones chips kept as souvenirs, career

20: Terry Sawchuk, 1949–50 to 1969–70

Sawchuk suffered numerous injuries during his career. His battered right elbow was a ceaseless source of bone chips that were removed from his arm at the end of each season—about 60 in all. He kept 20 of the fragments in a jar that he displayed on his mantel. Sawchuk had another jar that contained his removed appendix, floating in formaldehyde.

Only goalie to suffer a heart attack and still finish the game

Bruce Gamble, Philadelphia, February 9, 1972

The Flyers goalie suffered a heart attack in the first period of a game against the Vancouver Canucks, yet remained in the net for the entire game, backstopping the Flyers to a 3–1 win. It was Gamble's last NHL game.

Only Hall of Fame goalie demoted to the minors in mid-career

Jacques Plante, NY Rangers, 1964–65

A few future Hall of Fame goalies agreed to take conditioning stints in the minors when rehabbing from an injury, but Plante is the only one who was sent there against his wishes. His 17-game stint in purgatory with the Baltimore Clippers of the American Hockey League in 1964–65 so humiliated Plante that he retired to take a job as a beer salesman. He would return to the NHL three seasons later with the St. Louis Blues where he won the Vezina Trophy with Glenn Hall.

CHAPTER 11

Mano-
a-mano

Between 1934–35, when the rule was introduced, and 2001–02, 770 penalty shots were called in NHL action. Who's faired better one-on-one? Goaltenders have averaged a 62 per cent success rate against shooters, who have scored just 288 goals. Obviously, this is not the 50–50 proposition most assume it to be.

Most penalty shots awarded, career

9: Pavel Bure, 1991–92 to 2001–02
8: Mario Lemieux, 1984–85 to 2001–02
The Breakaway Kid has gone one-on-one a record nine times, eclipsing Lemieux with his eighth and ninth penalty shots in 2001–02. Bure has scored on five of his nine attempts.

Most penalty-shot goals, career

6: Mario Lemieux, 1984–85 to 2001–02
Lemieux has been stopped only twice—by Bill Ranford and Dominik Hasek—on eight penalty shots, lowering the league-wide save average of 62 per cent to just 25 per cent.

Most penalty shots faced by a goaltender, career

12: Glenn Hall, 1952–53 to 1970–71
12: Kelly Hrudey, 1983–84 to 1997–98
Hrudey and Hall each faced an all-time high 12 shooters, but the hidden record is Hall's save percentage, 66 per cent, or eight stops in 12 attempts compared to Hrudey's six saves.

Most different teams played for by a goaltender in a penalty-shot situation, career

5: Sean Burke, 1987–88 to 2001–02
Of the seven teams in his playing career, Burke faced penalty shots with New Jersey, Hartford, Philadelphia, Florida and Phoenix. No penalty shots were called against Carolina and Vancouver while Burke was in the net.

Most penalty shots awarded league-wide, one season

40: 1999–2000
Every team except Boston and Calgary contributed to the record 40 shots awarded in 1999–2000. A few other marks were

established: goalies stopped an all-time league-high 24 shots; shooters scored a record 16 times (matched only by 1997–98); and for the first time in memory only one Canadian-born player, Brad Isbister, scored a penalty-shot goal.

Most penalty-shot goals by a shooter, one season
3: Pavel Bure, Vancouver, 1997–98
Bure scored against San Jose's Mike Vernon, Phoenix's Nikolai Khabibulin and Ottawa's Damian Rhodes.

Most penalty shots faced by a goaltender, one season
6: George Hainsworth, Toronto, 1934–35
5: Roy Worters, NY Americans, 1934–35
5: Curtis Joseph, Toronto, 2001–02
Trigger-happy officials awarded 29 penalty shots in 1934–35 (when the rule was instituted), 11 shots shared between Hainsworth and Worters, who stopped all shooters. Their perfect 11–0 record was aided by the old-time rule, which required a player to shoot from 38 feet out. On January 22, 2002, Joseph became only the third netminder in history to face five or more penalty shots in a season, when he stopped Calgary's Jarome Iginla. Cujo stonewalled four of five shooters in 2001–02.

Most penalty shots stopped, one season
ALL-TIME RECORD
6: George Hainsworth, Toronto, 1934–35
MODERN-DAY RECORD
4: Curtis Joseph, Toronto, 2001–02
4: Alan Bester, Toronto, 1988–89
A curious coincidence is that all three record-holders in this category are Toronto netminders.

Most penalty shots faced by a goaltender, one game

2: several goalies

No netminder has yet to have to face three free shots in a game.

Fastest game-winning penalty-shot goal

12 seconds: Maurice Richard, January 1, 1952

Richard scored at 00:12 of the first period on a penalty shot after Chicago's Jim Peters hooked Montreal's Bert Olmstead from behind. Montreal beat Chicago 3–0.

Players who scored first career goal on a penalty shot

PLAYER	TEAM	SEASON	OPPOSING GOALIE
Ralph Bowman	St. L	1934–35	Alex Connell
Phil Hoene	LA	1973–74	Cesare Maniago
Ilkka Sinsalo	Phi	1981–82	Paul Harrison
Reggie Savage	Wsh	1990–91	Jon Casey

Player who scored his last career goal on a penalty shot

King Clancy, Toronto, November 14, 1936

Clancy's final NHL goal in his 16-year Hall of Fame career was a penalty-shot marker against Chicago's Mike Karakas. Clancy was the first defenseman to score on a penalty shot.

Longest wait before an NHL franchise recorded its first penalty shot

829 games: New Jersey Devils, December 17, 1984

New Jersey recorded its first penalty shot in its 10th season (dating back to and including franchise locations in Kansas City and Colorado). Rocky Trottier scored on Edmonton's Andy Moog.

CHAPTER 12

Ice
time

Although Gordie Howe and Doug Jarvis are synonymous with games-played records (Howe leads all players with 1,767 games and Jarvis recorded 964 consecutive games), several other NHLers carry the torch in many unofficial categories. For example, Jarvis is no longer the NHL's official ironman, including playoff games. And who holds the regular-season mark for most games played?

Most frequently played number of games, career

1: Almost 300 players, 1917–18 to 2001–02

It makes sense when you think about. More NHLers have played one game than any other number.

Fewest games missed in 20-year span

20: Gordie Howe, 1949–50 to 1968–69
28: Larry Murphy, 1980–81 to 1999–2000

Let's raise a toast to two of the most indestructable players in hockey history. Howe, the Motown machine, skated in 1,390 of a possible 1,410 games over a 20-year span. Murphy appeared in 1,560 of a possible 1,588 games during his 20-year impersonation of a Cyborg.

Most consecutive games, career (incl. playoffs)

949: Garry Unger, 1967–68 to 1982–83

Doug Jarvis tops Unger 964 to 914 games in the regular-season count, but Unger never missed a playoff match during his string, combining 914 regular-season and 35 playoff games between February 24, 1968, and December 21, 1979. Jarvis missed four playoff games in 1979, interrupting his ironman streak at 362 games when the postseason is included.

Most consecutive games by a defenseman, career (incl. playoffs)

549: Tim Horton, 1949–50 to 1973–74

The crew-cutted muscle man played every game with Toronto in a seven-year span between February 11, 1961, and February 4, 1968, combining 486 regular-season and 63 playoff games.

Most consecutive games with one team

884: Steve Larmer, Chicago, 1982–83 to 1992–93

The steady winger played 11 complete seasons in a row with

Chicago from October 6, 1982, to April 15, 1993. Larmer's streak
ended after a salary dispute forced him to sit out the start of
1993–94. In November 1993, he was traded to the Rangers.

776: Craig Ramsay, Buffalo, 1971–72 to 1984–85

Ramsay played nine consecutive complete seasons with Buffalo
from March 27, 1973, to February 10, 1983.

Most consecutive games with one team (incl. playoffs)

905: Steve Larmer, Chicago, 1982–83 to 1992–93

Larmer missed two playoff games during his first full season in
1982–83 but didn't skip another Blackhawks game for the next
10 years, compiling a 900-game stretch of 804 regular-season
and 101 playoff matches.

Most games, one season

86: Jimmy Carson, Detroit, Los Angeles, 1992–93
86: Bob Kudelski, Ottawa, Florida, 1993–94

This pair locked up this record by staying healthy and being
traded in the NHL's only 84-game seasons. Carson played 52
games with Detroit and 34 games with Los Angeles; Kudelski
played 42 games with Ottawa and 44 games with Florida.

Most games, one season (incl. playoffs)

108: Trevor Linden, Vancouver, 1993–94
108: Luc Robitaille, Los Angeles, 1992–93
108: Mike Donnelly, Los Angeles, 1992–93

Each combined 84 regular-season and 24 playoff games in
setting their endurance records.

Most consecutive games without scoring a goal

252: Ken Daneyko, 1999–2000 to 2001–02

The slow-footed Daneyko was never much of an offensive

threat, but in his senior years he has become about as mobile
as a fireplug. Kenny D. has not scored in more than three
full seasons.

Most consecutive games without scoring a goal from
start of career
218: Terry Murray, 1972–73 to 1981–82
Murray, a one-time defenseman for California, Philadelphia
and Detroit, must have impressed his coaches with his
positional play. It certainly wasn't because of his scoring,
plus-minus figures or penalty stats. For example, in 58 games
with California (no powerhouse club), Murray recorded a
minus-43, less than a shot-per-game average and only
48 minutes in box time. In 1980–81, he played 71 games with
Philadelphia and finally scored a goal in his 219th game.
During 1981–82 with Washington, Murray was even hotter,
scoring three times.

Longest career without scoring a point
61 games: Gord Strate, Detroit, 1956–57 to 1958–59
43 games: Frank Peters, NY Rangers, 1930–31
Pointless may best describe Strate's NHL career.

Most games without scoring a goal, one season
81 games: Mike Rathje, San Jose, 2000–01
The hulking Sharks defenseman has shown little interest in
either shooting or scoring since joining the NHL in 1993–94,
averaging less than a shot a game and one goal every 38 games.

Most games without scoring a point, one season
61: Tyler Wright, Pittsburgh, 1998–99
Penguins coach Kevin Constantine couldn't figure out how to fit

Wright into his system and the third-line centre spent his entire 61-game season pointless, registering only 16 shots.

Most games without a playoff appearance, career

734: Guy Charron, 1969–70 to 1980–81
439: Scott Walker, 1994–95 to 2001–02

Charron is the runaway record holder in this category, nearly 300 games ahead of his closest rival.

Most games without winning the Stanley Cup, career

1,443: Dave Andreychuk, 1982–83 to 2001–02
1,437: Phil Housley, 1982–83 to 2001–02

Ironically, Andreychuk and Housley both broke into the NHL in the same season with the Sabres. Since being traded by the Sabres, their paths of futility have led them no further than one finals series: Housley's close-but-no-cigar campaign with Washington in 1997–98.

Most games appeared in by two brothers, career

2,361: Marty and Matt Pavelich

Marty played in 634 games, while Matt, an NHL official, worked 1,727 games.

Most games played by two brothers, career

2,234: Maurice and Henri Richard

Maurice played 978 games and Henri, 1,256 games, all with Montreal.

Most games played by two brothers, career (incl. playoffs)

2,547: Maurice and Henri Richard

The Rocket played a combined 1,111 games and the Pocket Rocket, 1,436 games, all with Montreal.

Most games played by brothers, career

4,994: Brian, Brent, Darryl, Duane, Rich and Ron Sutter

Brent played in 1,111 games; Brian in 779; Darryl in 406; Duane in 731; Rich in 874; and Ron in 1,093.

Most games played by brothers, career (incl. playoffs)

5,597: Brian, Brent, Darryl, Duane, Rich and Ron Sutter

Brent played in a combined 1,255 games; Brian in 844; Darryl in 457; Duane in 892; Rich in 952; and Ron in 1,197.

Most sets of brothers participating in one game

4: NY Rangers and Chicago, December 1, 1940

This 1940 clash between the Hawks and Rangers boasted a record four brother combinations, two for each team. New York iced Lynn and Muzz Patrick and Neil and Mac Colville, while Chicago countered with Max and Doug Bentley and Bob and Bill Carse. The final score was 4–1 in favour of Chicago.

Fewest games to score 50 goals from start of season
39: Wayne Gretzky, Edmonton, 1981–82
42: Wayne Gretzky, Edmonton, 1983–84

Only a handful of NHLers have scored 50 goals in less than 50 games. Gretzky holds down the top two spots and he is the only player to nail his 50th before New Year's. His record-setting 50th was scored into an empty net in his 39th game on December 30, 1981, against Philadelphia.

Fewest games to score 100 points from start of season
34: Wayne Gretzky, Edmonton, 1983–84

The Great One hit the century mark in his 34th game on December 18, 1983.

Fewest games to score 100 points by a defenseman from start of season

57: Bobby Orr, Boston, 1974–75
58: Bobby Orr, Boston, 1970–71
59: Paul Coffey, Edmonton, 1985–86

Orr posted six 100-point seasons. He reached the milestone the fastest in his 57th game of the 1974–75 season on February 13, 1975. How quick is that? Only eight forwards in history have reached 100 points in fewer games.

Fewest games to score 100 goals from start of career

129: Mike Bossy, NY Islanders, 1978–79
130: Teemu Selanne, Winnipeg, 1993–94

After his astonishing 76-goal rookie season in 1992–93, it looked like Selanne had this record bagged. He needed just 24 more goals in 45 games to beat Bossy's 100-goals-in-129-games mark. But the Finnish Flash's season ended prematurely with a torn Achilles tendon. He scored just 25 times in his sophomore year, his 100th recorded in his 130th game, just one more game than Bossy. Bossy scored his 100th on February 19, 1979; Selanne on January 12, 1994.

Most games in a 100-goal career

1,244: Allan Stanley, 1948–49 to 1968–69

A defensive stalwart with five NHL teams, Stanley scored goals at a snail's pace: a perfect 100 in 21 seasons.

Fewest games to score 100 goals by a defenseman from start of career

300: Paul Coffey, Edmonton, 1983–84

Coffey netted his 100th goal in his 300th game, a 6–5 win against Winnipeg on February 27, 1984. He was in his fourth NHL season.

Fewest games to score 500 goals

575: Wayne Gretzky, 1979–80 to 1998–99
605: Mario Lemieux, 1984–85 to 2001–02

Just 30 games separate their marks. Gretzky scored his 500th on November 22, 1986; Lemieux on October 26, 1995.

Most games to score 500 goals

1,370: Johnny Bucyk, 1955–56 to 1977–78
1,285: Pat Verbeek, 1982–83 to 2001–02

No one has taken longer to reach the 500-goal mark than Bucyk. It's a record of patience. Verbeek, who ranks second in this category, trails Bucyk by more than a season's worth of games. Bucyk scored his 500th on October 30, 1975; Verbeek on March 22, 2000.

Fewest games by a 500-goal scorer, career

752: Mike Bossy, NY Islanders, 1977–78 to 1986–87

Bossy scored 573 goals in 752 games, his Hall of Fame career cut short by too many cross-checks across the back.

Fewest games to score 1,000 points

424: Wayne Gretzky, 1979–80 to 1998–99
513: Mario Lemieux, 1984–85 to 2001–02

Gretzky had a better supporting cast to reach 1,000 points than Lemieux and that difference may be what separates these record leaders by only 89 games.

Most games to score 1,000 points

1,308: Dale Hunter, 1980–81 to 1998–99
1,275: Pat Verbeek, 1982–83 to 2001–02

Seldom does box time help establish an offensive record, but for Hunter (3,565 penalty minutes) and Verbeek

(2,833 penalty minutes), their totals turned the journey into an unofficial record.

Fewest games to score 1,000 points by a defenseman

770: Paul Coffey, 1980–81 to 2000–01

To appreciate Coffey's point pace, consider that Jaromir Jagr took only seven fewer games to reach the 1,000-point mark. In fact, only 11 forwards scored their 1,000th point faster than Coffey, while the remaining 52 players, including five defensemen, were slower.

Most games to score 1,000 points by a defenseman

1,228: Larry Murphy, 1980–81 to 2000–01

Murphy spent 16 seasons with five teams before celebrating his 1,000th career point, the slowest among all six 1,000-point D-men.

Fewest games by 1,000-point players, career
752: Mike Bossy, 1977–78 to 1986–87

In his 10-season career, the Islanders' sniper scored at a sizzling pace. He notched 1,126 points in 752 games.

Most seasons leading a team in scoring

19: Wayne Gretzky, 1979–80 to 1998–99

With the exception of an injury-plagued 1992–93, Gretzky led his team in scoring every season during his 20-year career.

Most seasons leading a team in scoring by a defenseman

5: Ray Bourque, 1979–80 to 2000–01

Bourque's vision and scoring touch outclassed many forwards, including some on his own team. He led his middle-of-the-pack Bruins a record five times: 1984–85 (86 points), 1986–87 (95), 1987–88 (81), 1990–91 (94) and 1991–92 (81).

Highest percentage of games a point was scored

82%: Wayne Gretzky, 1979–80 to 1998–99

Gretzky scored at least one point in every four of five games; officially 2,857 points in 1,487 games.

Highest goals-per-game average, career (min. 200 goals)

.805: Mario Lemieux, 1984–85 to 2001–02
.762: Mike Bossy, 1977–78 to 1986–87
.756: Cy Denneny, 1917–18 to 1928–29

Lemieux leads all NHL scorers with an .805 average on 654 goals in 812 games. Even as he slows down this mark should last awhile.

Highest games-per-goals ratio, career

47.2 games: Brad Marsh, 1978–79 to 1992–93
37.7 games: Ken Daneyko, 1983–84 to 2001–02
35.5 games: Luke Richardson, 1987–88 to 2001–02

Daneyko and Richardson are slowly chasing down Marsh in this turtle derby. Marsh scored 23 goals in 1,086 games. Daneyko has scored 34 times in 1,214 games. Richardson has 31 goals in 1,101 games.

Highest points-per-games ratio, career (min. 200 goals)

1.98: Mario Lemieux, 1984–85 to 2001–02
1.92: Wayne Gretzky, 1979–80 to 1998–99
1.50: Mike Bossy, 1977–78 to 1986–87

Lemieux set a few NHL records that were out of Gretzky's reach, including his 1.98 average on 1,604 points in 809 games.

Highest games-per-point ratio, career (min. 1,000 games)

7.8 games: Ken Daneyko, 1983–84 to 2001–02

The opposition end of the ice is foreign territory for Daneyko. The stay-at-home New Jersey Devils rearguard has recorded only 169 points in 1,214 career regular-season games, a lowly average of one point for every 7.8 games.

Longest time between NHL goals

14 years: Fred Hucul, 1950–51 to 1967–68

After scoring for Chicago in 1952–53, Hucul ended up on the side of a milk carton for 740 games in the minors. Traded for cash by a few clubs, his next NHL stop came 14 years later with St. Louis where he scored two goals in 1967–68.

Longest time between NHL goals for the same team

16 years: Randy Cunneyworth, 1981–82 to 1998–99

Cunneyworth did not score a goal for Buffalo from November 15, 1981 to February 11, 1999. Between that time he potted 185 goals in 831 games on five NHL teams. His first and last NHL goals came with Buffalo.

Longest time between NHL hat tricks

11 years: Dit Clapper, 1932–33 to 1944–45

It took Boston great Dit Clapper exactly 11 years, 345 days to repeat a hat trick, from March 9, 1933 to February 17, 1945.

Most consecutive games scoring or assisting on consecutive goals

15: Jaromir Jagr, Pittsburgh, 1999–2000

This is a record that deserves more attention. Was Jagr central to Pittsburgh's attack or what? The Czech locomotive scored or assisted on 15 consecutive Penguins goals from October 16 to

November 4, 1999. He counted seven goals and eight assists during his streak.

Most NHL teams, career

10: Michel Petit, 1982–83 to 1997–98
10: Jean-Jacques Daigneault, 1984–85 to 2000–01
During his 16-year career, Petit played in 827 games for Vancouver, NY Rangers, Quebec, Toronto, Calgary, Los Angeles, Tampa Bay, Edmonton, Philadelphia and Phoenix. Five of the 10 teams traded Petit to another team in mid-season—another league record. Daigneault played 899 games for Vancouver, Philadelphia, Montreal, St. Louis, Pittsburgh, Anaheim, NY Islanders, Nashville, Phoenix and Minnesota. He was traded mid-season five times, including 1995–96, when he made three moves: from Montreal to St. Louis to Pittsburgh.

Most teams by a goaltender, career

8: Gary Smith, 1965–66 to 1979–80
8: Ron Tugnutt, 1987–88 to 2001–02
These two goalies played for more than half the number of teams in the NHL. Smith, a good goalie when given some talent up front, earned the nickname "Suitcase" by making the rounds with eight clubs: Toronto, Oakland (which later became California), Chicago, Vancouver, Washington, Minnesota and Winnipeg. Tugnutt, another journeyman loved by his long-distance mover, made it eight with Dallas in 2002. His previous pit stops included Quebec, Edmonton, Anaheim, Montreal, Ottawa, Pittsburgh and Columbus.

Most Original Six teams, career

6: Vic Lynn, 1942–43 to 1953–54
Lynn is the only NHLer to suit up for all teams of the Original

Six. He played with NY Rangers (one game), Montreal (two games), Detroit (three games), Chicago (40 games), Boston (68 games) and Toronto (213 games).

Most teams, 20-goal season
6: Ray Sheppard, 1987–88 to 1999–2000
5: several players, including Dean Prentice and Eddie Shack
Sheppard scored 20 goals with six teams: Carolina, Florida, NY Rangers, Buffalo, Detroit and San Jose.

Most teams, 30-goal season
5: Mike Gartner, 1979–80 to 1997–98
The model of reliability, Gartner scored 30 goals with five teams: Washington, Minnesota, NY Rangers, Toronto and Phoenix.

Most teams played for by brothers as teammates
4: Des and Earl Roche, 1930–31 to 1934–35
In their four NHL seasons, Des and Earl moved together from team to team with more consistency than any other two NHLers in league history. The brothers played for four different clubs together: Montreal Maroons, Ottawa, St. Louis Eagles and Detroit.

Most teams, one season
4: Dennis O'Brien, Minnesota, Colorado, Cleveland, Boston, 1977–78
4: Dave McLlwain, Winnipeg, Buffalo, NY Islanders, Toronto, 1991–92
O'Brien and McLlwain are the only NHLers to have played with four teams in one season. McLlwain owns another record in this category: he is the only player to have played for a team in four divisions in one season. Winnipeg was in the Smythe Division; Buffalo in the Adams; the Islanders in the Patrick; and Toronto in the Norris.

CHAPTER 13

Team wonders and blunders

The number 446 holds a special place in the NHL record books for two teams in the category of season-goal totals. The Edmonton Oilers and Washington Capitals both figure prominently in the equation, with the remarkable performance of one club countering the abysmal showing of the other. It's an easy ID, unless you've been living under a rock.

Oldest NHL team still in existence
Montreal Canadiens, 1917–18
In its first season, the NHL iced four teams: the Montreal
Canadiens, Toronto Arenas, Montreal Wanderers and Ottawa
Senators (the club that folded in 1933–34).

Oldest hockey team name still in existence
Ottawa Senators
The Ottawa Silver Seven became the Ottawa Senators in 1906.
They won their first Stanley Cup as the Senators in 1908–09, the
season prior to the founding of the Montreal Canadiens, and
nine years before the NHL was formed.

Most famous team nicknames
The Flying Frenchmen: Montreal Canadiens
The Broad Street Bullies: Philadelphia Flyers
The Broadway Blueshirts: NY Rangers
The Canadiens earned their famed moniker (as well as "the Habs")
with the firewagon play of speedsters Howie Morenz and Aurel Joliat.
Later, with Maurice Richard and Jean Béliveau, the Canadiens—in
their celebrated red uniforms with the famous "CH" crest—were the
team to beat. Philadelphia's nickname grew out of the rough and
tumble game the Flyers employed to win two Stanley Cups during the
1970s. Their home rink, the Spectrum, was on South Broad Street.
The Rangers' moniker was a natural one for a team that wore blue
uniforms and whose home rink was located near one of the world's
most famous avenues.

Most games by an NHL team

5,382: Montreal Canadiens, 1917–18 to 2001–02

The Canadiens' history predates the formation of the NHL in
1917–18. It's the only team remaining from the original four
NHL franchises.

Fewest games by an NHL team

4: Montreal Wanderers, 1917–18

The Wanderers withdrew from the league after fire claimed
their home rink, the Montreal Arena. Although the team had
only played four games, it was credited with two default losses,
making its record 1–5–0.

Most man-games lost to injury, one season

536 games: Montreal Canadiens, 1999–2000
531 games: Montreal Canadiens, 2000–01

Was it old Montreal Forum ghosts, the Molson Centre's rigid
boards and seamless glass, or lack of training and conditioning?
No team has suffered through more man-games lost; and Montreal did it in consecutive years. It's gotta be the disgruntled
spirits of dynasties past.

Most geographically misplaced team in an NHL division

Vancouver Canucks, 1970–71 to 1973–74

Vancouver spent its first four NHL seasons in the East Division,
battling teams that were based more than 3,000 miles away.

Highest average attendance by an expansion team

18,337 fans: Minnesota Wild, 2001–02
17,205 fans: Atlanta Thrashers, 1999–2000

The Wild finished with 68 points, the seventh highest point total
for an expansion team, but they clearly won at the box office,

averaging 18,337 fans per game in their first season, including 41 sellouts at the Xcel Energy Center. Atlanta recorded 14 sellouts, while getting thrashed in the win column, 14–61–7, the fourth-worst by an expansion club since 1970.

Fewest season-ticket holders, one season
500: Chicago Blackhawks, 1956–57
Although the six-team era (1942–1967) is remembered as a golden age, it wasn't so golden for everyone. In 1956–57, last-place Chicago had only 500 season-ticket holders and drew less than 7,000 fans per game. Seat prices were clearly not the cause of the fans' indifference, as they ranged from a very affordable $1.25 to $4.00. The problem was the Blackhawks' awful ineptitude. Even with only six teams in the league, making the playoffs was an impossible task. In the 12-year span between 1944–45 and 1957–58, Chicago finished last nine times and made the postseason only once. In 1950–51, the Hawks finished a distant 65 points out of first.

Highest home winning-percentage by a guest singer
.796: Kate Smith, Philadelphia Flyers
The Flyers first played a recording of Kate Smith singing "God Bless America" in place of the national anthem before a game with Toronto on December 11, 1969. The Flyers won 6–3 and from that point on Smith became the club's good-luck charm. In all, the Flyers posted a 63–15–3 record in games when Smith's booming voice was heard over the Spectrum's loudspeakers.

Most goals, one season
446: Edmonton Oilers, 1983–84
426: Edmonton Oilers, 1985–86

424: Edmonton Oilers, 1982–83
417: Edmonton Oilers, 1981–82
401: Edmonton Oilers, 1984–85
Few teams, including the Oilers (except in these offensive totals), own bragging rights to the top five places in any record. No team has ever embarrassed as many opponents as the Gretzky-led Oilers did during the 1980s.

Most goals allowed, one season
446: Washington Capitals, 1974–75
415: Detroit Red Wings, 1985–86
414: San Jose Sharks, 1992–93
In 1974–75, Washington registered the same goal total as the 1983–84 Oilers. The only problem for the Capitals was that their record related to goals allowed. They gave up seven double-digit games (4–10, 1–11, 1–12, 0–10, 3–10, 1–12 and 2–10).

Most goals by an expansion team
303: Hartford Whalers, 1979–80
301: Edmonton Oilers, 1979–80
Imported from the WHA, the Whalers iced veterans Gordie and Mark Howe, Dave Keon, Bobby Hull and two 100-point players in Mike Rogers and Blaine Stoughton. Among expansion teams starting from scratch, Tampa Bay registered the most in its debut: 245 goals in 1992–93.

Most times one team led the NHL in both goals for and goals against, one season
2: Chicago Blackhawks, 1926–27 and 1947–48
The Blackhawks are the only team on record to lead in goals for and goals against in the same season. They did it twice: in 1926–27 when they recorded league-highs of 115 goals scored

and 116 goals allowed; and in 1947–48 when they scored 195 goals and gave up 225 goals.

Most goals scored in the final minute of play to produce a win

3: Montreal Maroons, March 15, 1932
3: Dallas Stars, October 14, 1995

In the dying moments of a 3–1 game against the New York Rangers, the Maroons ripped three quick goals with two Rangers in the penalty box as Hooley Smith, Dave Trottier and Babe Siebert scored at 19:12, 19:20 and 19:36 to salt a 4–3 win. In October 1995, Dallas stung Boston three times in the final minute at 19:11, 19:44 and 19:55 to beat the Bruins 6–5.

Fewest defending players on the ice during a power play

2: Toronto, November 20, 1928

Until 1956–57, players had to serve the full duration of their minor penalties even if a power-play marker was scored. This led to some ridiculous situations, none more absurd than a game in 1928–29, when Toronto goalie Lorne Chabot and centre Andy Blair faced five Ottawa Senators with four of their mates in the penalty box. Ottawa's King Clancy scored on the four-man advantage.

Most empty-net goals allowed by a winning team, one game

2: NY Rangers, April 5, 1970

New York led Detroit 9–3 in the last game of the 1969–70 season, when Rangers coach Emile Francis pulled his goalie for an extra attacker in the third period. Francis hadn't lost his mind: he was trying to score another goal to boost his club's chances of making the playoffs. In the event that New York and Montreal finished in a tie, the final playoff berth would go to the team with the most goals. The move bombed: Gordie Howe and Nick Libbet scored into the empty Rangers net.

Most empty-net goals scored, one game
5: Chicago Blackhawks, April 5, 1970
Chicago scored five empty-net goals against Montreal, who, facing elimination from the playoffs, yanked Rogie Vachon regularly during the last eight-and-a-half minutes of the third period to try to score three goals it needed to qualify for the postseason.

Most icing calls against one team, one game
87: Boston Bruins, December 3, 1931
On November 8, 1931, the New York Americans defended a 3–2 lead against Boston by repeatedly icing the puck. Bruins president Charles Adams was so upset by the tactic that he ordered his team to return the favour when the teams met again on December 3. The result was a tedium-inducing 0–0 draw that saw Boston ice the puck a record 87 times.

Fewest goals allowed, one season
OLD-TIME RECORD
42: Ottawa Senators, 1925–26 (in 36 games)
43: Montreal Canadiens, 1928–29 (in 44 games)
MODERN-DAY RECORD (MIN. 70-GAME SCHEDULE)
131: Toronto Maple Leafs, 1953–54
131: Montreal Canadiens, 1955–56
132: Detroit Red Wings, 1953–54

Fewest goals scored by an expansion team (since 1967–68)
153: Oakland Seals, 1967–68
168: Minnesota Wild, 2000–01
In a year when a record six franchises joined the NHL, Oakland assembled the worst expansion team with a record 15–42–17.

Only Minnesota (and their stifling defensive system under trap-guru coach Jacques Lemaire) had a comparable expansion season, although Lemaire knew what he was doing and got a respectable 25–39–13–5.

Lowest goals-per-game average, one season

ALL-TIME RECORD

0.75: Chicago Blackhawks, 1928–29, in 44 games
1.05: Pittsburgh Pirates, 1928–29, in 44 games
1.20: New York Americans, 1928–29, in 44 games
The 1928–29 season marked the historical nadir of NHL scoring. Chicago scored just 33 times that year.

MODERN-DAY RECORD

1.84: Tampa Bay Lightning, 1997–98, in 82 games
1.90: Chicago Blackhawks, 1953–54, in 70 games
If not for the awful ineptitude of Tampa Bay's team in 1997–98, Chicago would own the modern-day record as well.

Largest plus-margin between goals for and goals against, one season

Plus-216 goals: Montreal Canadiens, 1976–77
Montreal scored 387 goals and allowed just 171. They also earned the all-time best plus-differential: 2.70, based on 4.84 goals for per game versus 2.14 goals against per game.

Largest minus-margin between goals for and goals against, one season

Minus-265 goals: Washington Capitals, 1974–75
The Caps scored 181 goals but allowed 446. They also earned the league's worst differential in modern times: 3.32, based on 2.26 goals for per game versus 5.58 goals against per game.

Fastest five goals allowed by one team
2 minutes, 7 seconds: St. Louis Blues, November 22, 1972

Depending on your point of view, St. Louis goalie Wayne Stephenson either produced an NHL record or allowed Pittsburgh an NHL record: the fastest five-goal rampage by one team, all of them coming between 12:00 and 14:07 of the third period in a 10–4 stomping of the Blues.

Fewest shots on goal in a game

6: Toronto Maple Leafs, May 8, 2000
7: Washington Capitals, February 12, 1978

These records couldn't have produced positive results: Toronto was beaten 3–0 by New Jersey; the Caps lost 4–1 to Philadelphia.

Fewest shots on goal by a winning team

9: San Jose Sharks, November 4, 1998
9: Toronto Maple Leafs, March 4, 1999

It's weird enough that a team could win with only nine shots on net, but how about it happening twice in the same season by identical 4–0 scores? That's what took place exactly four months apart in 1998–99. The Sharks scored three times in six shots on Dallas's Ed Belfour and once in three shots on his replacement, Roman Turek. The Stars got nothing past Mike Vernon in 21 shots. In the second game, the Leafs scored three in five shots on St. Louis rookie Brent Johnson, and one in four shots on his replacement Jim Carey. Curtis Joseph picked up the shutout against the Blues, stopping 28 shots.

Most consecutive seasons leading in goals scored

10: Montreal Canadiens

The organization that general manager Frank Selke began

building in the 1940s produced a goal-scoring powerhouse in the 1950s and 1960s. In every season from 1953–54 to 1962–63, the Flying Frenchmen led the league in goals, amassing a 10-year count of 2,356 goals.

Most teammates ranked consecutively atop the scoring race, one season

4: Boston Bruins, 1970–71 and 1973–74

Only twice have teammates finished first, second, third and fourth place in the NHL's top-10. Both times Boston recorded this scoring anomaly. In 1970–71 with Phil Esposito (152 points), Bobby Orr (139), Johnny Bucyk (116) and Ken Hodge (105); and in 1973–74 with Esposito (145 points), Orr (122), Hodge (105) and Wayne Cashman (89).

Most top-10 scorers on one team, one season
7: Boston Bruins 1970–71

Some teams have fielded five top-10 players in a season, but only the Bruins placed seven among the elite circle: Phil Esposito, Bobby Orr, Johnny Buyck, Ken Hodge, Wayne Cashman, Johnny McKenzie and Fred Stanfield (tied for 10th spot).

Most 50-goal scorers on one team, one season

3: Edmonton Oilers, 1983–84 and 1985–86

The Oilers iced the only team blessed with three 50-goal scorers in a single season and they pulled it off twice. In 1983–84 with Wayne Gretzky (87 goals), Glenn Anderson (54) and Jari Kurri (52); and in 1985–86 with Jari Kurri (68 goals), Glenn Anderson (54) and Wayne Gretzky (52).

Most players who scored 50th goals on one team

7: Pittsburgh Penguins
7: Calgary Flames
6: Montreal, Detroit, Philadelphia, Los Angeles

Pittsburgh and Calgary lead with seven 50-goal scorers after the Penguins' Jaromir Jagr did it in 1995–96 and the Flames' Jarome Iginla in 2001–02.

Most 100-point scorers on one team, one season

4: Boston Bruins, 1970–71
4: Edmonton, 1982–83; 1983–84; 1985–86
4: Pittsburgh, 1992–93

Most 500-goal scorers on one team, one season

4: Detroit Red Wings, 2001–02

Detroit is the only NHL team to ice four 500-goal scorers in one season: Steve Yzerman, Brett Hull, Luc Robitaille and Brendan Shanahan.

Most players who scored 500th goals on one team

5: Detroit Red Wings

Brendan Shanahan's 500th goal in 2001–02 earned Detroit this record, as the fifth 500-goal player on one team. Gordie Howe, Dino Ciccarelli, Steve Yzerman and Pat Verbeek all recorded No. 500 with the Red Wings.

Highest goals-per-game average by all teams, one season

ALL-TIME RECORD
10.05 goals: 1917–18

More than ten goals per game were scored in the 20-game schedule. It was the NHL's first season.

8.17 goals: 1943–44
8.03 goals: 1981–82
The only two years in modern times the league averaged eight goals per game.

Lowest goals-per-game average by all teams, one season

2.92 goals: 1928–29
It was goalie heaven and the last season before forward passing was permitted in all three zones.

4.79 goals: 1952–53
In consecutive seasons the NHL recorded the only numbers below five-goals-per-game in modern times. In 1952–53 and 1953–54, there were 1,006 and 1,009 goals in 210 games.

Largest margin in penalty minutes over second-place team, one season

694: Philadelphia Flyers, 1974–75
640: Philadelphia Flyers, 1980–81
The brutality of the City of Brotherly Love's 1975 Cup-winning team is underlined by this startling stat. The St. Louis Blues, the NHL's second-highest penalized team in 1974–75, was not even in stick-throwing range. The Flyers amassed 1,969 minutes, the Blues had 1,275. In 1980–81, the Flyers led the second-place Rangers 2,621 minutes to 1,981.

Most 300-penalty-minute players on one team, one season

3: Buffalo Sabres, 1991–92
The Sabres set an NHL record for team penalty totals (2,713 min-

utes) in 1991–92 due in large part to the testosterone-fuelled play of Rob Ray (354 minutes), Gord Donnelly (316 minutes) and Brad May (309 minutes), the only 300-minute trio in league annals.

Most teammates to finish among the top five penalty-minute leaders, one season
4: Philadelphia Flyers, 1972–73
The Flyers iced four of the top five penalty leaders in 1972–73, a wake-up call to where hockey was heading, at least temporarily. Dave Schultz (259 minutes) finished first, Bob Kelly (238) second, Andre Dupont (215) fourth and Don Saleski (205) fifth.

Best penalty-killing percentage, one season
89.3 per cent: Dallas Stars, 1999–2000
The Stars allowed just 33 power-play goals in 307 shorthanded situations, eclipsing the previous high of 89.2, set by Boston in 1998–99 and Washington in 1997–98.

Most consecutive penalty kills, one season
53: Washington Capitals, 1999–2000
Washington killed off 53 straight man-disadvantage situations from October 26 to November 24, 1999, and tied another record by going 12 straight games without allowing a power-play goal.

Most penalty-free games by one team, one season
5: Detroit Red Wings, 1936–37
This Wings squad was a docile bunch. Eleven of its regulars collected 20 minutes or less in box time. Team points leader Marty Barry finished with just six penalty minutes and won the Lady Byng Trophy as the year's most gentlemanly player.

Lowest average of penalty minutes per game, one season

4.1 minutes: Boston Bruins, 1943–44
4.8 minutes: New York Americans, 1939–40
4.8 minutes: New York Americans, 1940–41
4.8 minutes: Chicago Blackhawks, 1943–44

The most gentlemanly teams in NHL history played in the early 1940s. The 1943–44 Bruins compiled only 207 PIM in 50 games.

Most consecutive seasons leading league in penalty minutes

11: Philadelphia Flyers, 1971–72 to 1981–82

No other team has come close to this mark. The Broad Street Bullies built an outlaw empire based on intimidation.

Longest reign of a team penalty-minutes record

42 years: Montreal Maroons, 1926–27 to 1968–69

The 1926–27 Maroons were a nasty crew. Just how nasty is evident when you consider they racked up 716 penalty minutes in a 44-game schedule. Four of the club's players—Nels Stewart, Babe Siebert, Red Dutton and Reg Noble—broke the 100-PIM mark, a rarity in that era. The record stood until 1947–48, when Toronto surpassed it in the 60-game sked, with 758 PIM. Even so, the Maroons' average of 16.3 minutes of box time per game was four more than the Leafs averaged. It wasn't until 1968–69, when the bad-ass Bruins swaggered onto the scene, that another team finally topped the Maroons' mark, a span of 42 years.

CHAPTER 14

In a
league of
their own

Decades apart, the best winning

seasons in NHL history were coached

by one man: Scotty Bowman. Under Bowman,

Montreal earned a record 60 wins in 1976–77.

He topped that team mark with Detroit's 62-win

season during 1995–96. A first- and second-place

ranking, 19 seasons apart. Bowman's amazing feat

stands alone.

Most consecutive first-place finishes

7: Detroit Red Wings, 1948–49 to 1954–55

Like Montreal's streak of five Stanley Cups, this mark appears beyond the reach of mortals. The Gordie Howe-led Red Wings soared above the pack for seven straight seasons.

Most consecutive last-place finishes
5: Boston Bruins, 1960–61 to 1964–65

Until Bobby Orr changed their fortunes, the bumbling Bruins were mired in the muck of the Original Six basement.

Most last-place finishes

12: Chicago Blackhawks, 1927–28 to 1956–57

Until Bobby Hull and Stan Mikita blew into the Windy City, Chicago was a disaster zone. Two Cups in the 1930s can't hide a record 12 seasons in the cellar between 1927–28 and 1956–57.

Most consecutive losing seasons

13: Kansas City/Colorado/New Jersey, 1974–75 to 1986–87

Despite two franchise moves, three name changes and three different home towns spread across the continent, the Scouts, Rockies and Devils didn't ice a winning team until 1987–88, when New Jersey finally notched a 38–36–6 record.

Most wins by an expansion team

33: Florida Panthers, 1993–94

An 84-game schedule, coach Roger Neilson's defensive system, a few tough, reliable veterans and the stellar goaltending of John Vanbiesbrouck aided Florida in achieving this mark.

Fewest wins, one season

4: Quebec Bulldogs, 1919–20 (in 24 games)
4: Philadelphia Quakers, 1930–31 (in 44 games)

MODERN-DAY RECORD (MIN. 70-GAME SCHEDULE)

8: Washington Capitals, 1974–75
9: Winnipeg Jets, 1980–81

All these teams were hopeless. Washington won seven at home and one on the road, an average of one win every 10 excruciating games.

Fewest losses, one season

ALL-TIME RECORD

5: Ottawa Senators, 1919–20 (in 24 games)
5: Boston Bruins, 1929–30 (in 44 games)
5: Montreal Canadiens, 1943–44 (in 50 games)

MODERN-DAY RECORD (MIN. 70-GAME SCHEDULE)

8: Montreal Canadiens, 1976–77
10: Montreal Canadiens, 1972–73
10: Montreal Canadiens, 1977–78

Bowman. Bowman. Bowman. Every year. But look at his team: Ken Dryden, Guy Lafleur, Larry Robinson, Jacques Lemaire and Bob Gainey.

Most losses, one season

71: San Jose Sharks, 1992–93
70: Ottawa Senators, 1992–93

A very bad year for first- and second-year clubs, as weak sisters San Jose and Ottawa struggled through miserable 24-point seasons. Their opponents in 1992–93 set an NHL record for most 100-point teams in a season with seven.

Most points by an expansion team
83: Florida Panthers, 1993–94
Masterminded by general manager Bill Torrey, the Panthers' Cinderella team came within one point of making the postseason, and set an NHL points record among expansion clubs.

Best winning percentage by an expansion team
ALL-TIME RECORD
.636: NY Rangers, 1926–27
.542: Pittsburgh Pirates, 1925–26
The Rangers were bolstered by stars from their western pro leagues such as Frank Boucher and Bill Cook. Pittsburgh, a former amateur champion, was led by future Hall of Famers Lionel Conacher and Roy Worters.

MODERN-DAY RECORD
.494: Florida Panthers, 1993–94
Florida accrued the best modern-day winning percentage on record with 33 wins, 34 losses and 17 ties.

Fewest points, one season
ALL-TIME RECORD
8: Quebec Bulldogs, 1919–20
Quebec won four and lost 20 in a 24-game schedule

MODERN-DAY RECORD (MIN. 70-GAME SCHEDULE)
21: Washington Capitals, 1974–75
Just two seasons before Montreal established their 132-point league standard of 60–8–12, Washington set an NHL low of 8–67–5, winning the same number of games as Montreal had lost all season.

Most points by a non-playoff team, one season

92: Montreal Canadiens, 1969–70

92: Edmonton Oilers, 2001–02

The 1969–70 season was a hiccup year for Montreal. Amidst the great dynasty teams of the 1960s and 1970s, this was merely a good team. Tied with the fourth-place Rangers in almost every category, including wins, losses, ties and total points, Montreal (38–22–16) settled for fifth with two less goals, 244 to 246. Its playoff hopes dashed in the Eastern Conference, Montreal still finished six points ahead of playoff-bound St. Louis, leaders in the Western Conference. The Habs' 38–22–16 season also established this best winning percentage (.605) by a non-playoff team on record. Edmonton's failure to make the playoffs was due to stiff competition in the Western Conference.

Fewest points by a playoff team, one season

MODERN-DAY RECORD (MIN.70-GAME SCHEDULE)

52: Toronto Maple Leafs, 1987–88

How could a team lose 49 games in an 80-game schedule and still get into the playoffs? The 21-team NHL had four divisions and a first-versus-fourth, second-versus-third playoff format for each division. With no interlocking match-ups between divisions, Toronto's 52 points (21–49–10) gave it fourth place in the weak Norris Division. The Maple Leafs finished 30 points back of the non-playoff Rangers, an 82-point team in the Patrick Division. Toronto also claims the all-time record for worst winning percentage (.325) by a non-playoff team.

Largest single-season increase in winning percentage (min. 44 games)

.345: San Jose Sharks, 1993–94
.330: Montreal Canadiens, 1943–44

The Sharks awakened from their 24-point slumber in 1992–93 to flash 82 points on the board in 1993–94. Having two-thirds of the great Soviet KLM line in Igor Larionov and Sergei Makarov helped, but hard-nosed coach Kevin Constantine lit the fire.

Largest single-season decline in winning percentage

.325: NY Rangers, 1941–42
.295: Ottawa Senators, 1929–30

After finishing first in 1941–42, the Rangers ship sank to the bottom of the sea, decimated by the loss of key players to the war effort. Ottawa suffered the consequences of foolishly trading its best player, King Clancy, to Toronto.

Best home-ice winning percentage, one season

.955: Boston Bruins, 1929–30

Led by defenseman Eddie Shore and the high-scoring Dynamite Line of Dit Clapper, Cooney Weiland and Dutch Gainor, Boston finished first overall in the 10-team NHL, 26 points ahead of its nearest rival. They won 21 games and lost only one at the Boston Garden to earn the league's all-time best winning percentage on home ice.

Best road winning percentage, one season

.795: Boston Bruins, 1929–30

Boston may have been virtually unbeatable in the confines of

Boston Garden but the club was no slouch on the road either, posting an away mark of 17 wins, four losses and one tie.

Largest single-season improvement in points
58: San Jose Sharks, 1993–94

Up was the only way to go after a disastrous 24-point year in 1992–93. Even so, rookie coach Kevin Constantine looked like a miracle worker after engineering this record rise to 82 points.

Largest single-season decline in points
40: Detroit Red Wings, 1970–71
38: Chicago Blackhawks, 1953–54

The NHL's top scoring line of Alex Delvecchio, Gordie Howe and Frank Mahovlich led the Wings to a 95-point season in 1969–70. The next year, 1970–71, Howe played his last season, Mahovlich was traded and new coaches (Ned Harkness, Doug Barkley) replaced the old guard (Bill Gadsby, Sid Abel). Detroit plunged to 55 points. Chicago recorded 69 points in 1952–53 and bottomed out with 31 points in 1953–54, a modern-day franchise low. So bad was their standing that the Blackhawks managed another dubious mark: most points behind a second last-place team. Chicago finished a record 37 points back of second-last place NY Rangers.

Largest point increases in second NHL season
26: Boston Bruins, 1925–26
26: NY Islanders, 1973–74

Almost a half-century apart, the Bruins and the Islanders made the NHL's biggest jumps by second-year teams, a forecast of future glory. Just three years after Boston's record rise, the Bruins won the Cup in 1928–29; the Islanders needed six more seasons to win their first of four-in-a-row in 1979–80.

Most shutouts by all teams, one season

186 shutouts: 2000–01

Defense rules. Buffalo recorded a league-high 13 shutouts (Dominik Hasek had 11) while the New York Rangers, with six different goalies, failed to contribute any zeroes to the cause.

184 shutouts: 2001–02

The year of the Quebecois netminders: Patrick Roy recorded a league-high nine shutouts; Jose Theodore, Patrick Lalime and Dan Cloutier had seven; and Jocelyn Thibault and Felix Potvin had six.

Highest percentage of NHL games that produced shutouts, one season

55%: 1928–29

Rules for forward passing (which discouraged offense) were changed the year after this record panicked league executives. There were a sleep-inducing 120 shutouts in 220 games.

Most consecutive shutouts from start of season

5: Toronto Maple Leafs, 1930–31

Goalies Lorne Chabot and Benny Grant deserve credit for the record zero streak but the acquisition of veteran defenseman King Clancy in 1930 cannot be underestimated. Clancy (purchased for an almost unheard sum of $35,000) proved his value immediately, as Toronto earned its five-game shutout run in Clancy's first five games, from November 12 to 22, 1930.

Most scoreless ties, one season

ALL-TIME RECORD

14: 1928–29

MODERN-DAY RECORD

7: 2000–01

Most scoreless ties by a team, one season
7: Ottawa Senators, 1927–28
Alex Connell logged 15 shutouts with eight wins and seven scoreless ties.

Most scoreless games without penalties
1: Chicago Blackhawks vs. Toronto Maple Leafs, February 20, 1944
No offensive stats were recorded except for a disallowed goal on a high stick. Bill Chadwick refereed the match, which was played at full tilt in under two hours.

Most games shutout, one season
ALL-TIME RECORD
20: Chicago Blackhawks, 1928–29
MODERN-DAY RECORD
13: Chicago Blackhawks, 1953–54
Chicago had a sick attraction for zeroes, setting both the old and new records. In 1953–54, the Hawks went scoreless in six at home and seven on the road.

Most consecutive games shutout
8: Chicago Blackhawks, 1928–29
The pitiful Hawks couldn't locate the net for almost a month. They lost eight straight games 1–0, 1–0, 1–0, 3–0, 3–0, 0–0, 3–0 and 0–0 from February 7 to 28, 1929.

Longest unbeaten streak on opening night
17 games: Montreal Canadiens, 1963–64 to 1979–80
Montreal shot out of the starting gate a record 17 straight seasons, going 13–0–4 on opening night.

Longest streak without a shorthanded goal

121 games: NY Rangers, April 11, 1997 to January 10, 1999

Strictly speaking, John MacLean's penalty-shot goal against Tampa Bay wasn't really in a shorthanded situation, but Ranger teammate Brent Fedyk was in the box for slashing during the MacLean goal. New York ended its streak and won 5–2.

Longest streak without a win against one opponent

34 games: Washington vs. Montreal, October 31, 1974 to February 19, 1980

If ever there was a team in need of a sports psychologist, it was Washington. It took six years and 34 games (0–31–3) before the Capitals got the Canadiens' monkey off their back. The sad facts: Washington was out scored by Montreal 195–55; and 11 of the 34 games were shutouts.

Longest streak without a road win against one opponent

35 games: Minnesota vs. Boston, November 29, 1967 to November 8, 1981

The North Stars got the cold sweats just flying into Logan Airport. Thirteen years elapsed before Minnesota won at the Boston Garden. The club was 0–28–7 over that span.

Longest road trip

11 games: Calgary Flames, 1987–88

Road warriors or road kill? During the 1988 Winter Olympics in Calgary, the Flames played a record 11 away games in a row, with a short respite at home (after three games) for the NHL All-Star break. The trip earned Calgary a franchise road record for regular-season play.

Longest uninterrupted road trip

18 days: San Jose Sharks, 1998–99

The jet-lagged Sharks played 10 road games in nine cities over four time zones from February 3 to 21, 1999. They completed the trip with a 4–5–1 record.

Largest points-span between first- and last-place teams, one season

95: Montreal (127) and Washington (32), 1975–76
95: Pittsburgh (119) and Ottawa/San Jose (24), 1992–93

These monstrous numbers offer gruesome evidence of just how pathetic some NHL expansion teams have been.

Largest points-span between first- and second-place teams, one season

27: Detroit (131) and Colorado (104), 1995–96, in 80 games
26: Boston (77) and Montreal/Mtl Maroons (51), 1929–30, in 44 games
25: Montreal (83) and Detroit (58), 1943–44, in 50 games

This 1995–96 Motown juggernaut posted a record 62 wins. Even so, Detroit was upset by Colorado in the Western Conference finals. The 1929–30 Bruins' margin of domination is even more impressive considering the schedule was only 44 games. Calculated over an 80-game slate, Boston would have finished 47 points ahead of its nearest rival. Like Detroit, the Bean-towners crashed and burned in the postseason, losing in the finals to the Canadiens.

CHAPTER 15

Bench
boss

For some silly reason coaches never warranted recognition as record holders. Why? Maybe, it's simply because it's the players who play the game. And why do teams earn records without giving a nod to the motivator behind the bench? Is the bench boss above some standard of flattery? Not in our book.

Most seasons

30: Scotty Bowman, 1967–68 to 2001–02

Sports Illustrated once named Bowman the greatest coach in professional sports. ESPN ranked him fourth among all-time greatest coaches. There's not much debate that he's numero uno in hockey.

Most consecutive seasons

20: Jack Adams, Detroit, 1927–28 to 1946–47

Adams's name is synonymous with the development of Detroit hockey. He joined the franchise in its second season as coach and general manager and over the next 35 years won 12 regular-season championships (including seven in a row from 1948–49 to 1954–55), seven Stanley Cup titles and guided Gordie Howe to stardom.

Most seasons with one team

20: Jack Adams, Detroit, 1927–28 to 1946–47
19: Al Arbour, NY Islanders, 1973–74 to 1993–94

Adams coached Detroit to a 413–390–161 record in 964 games. Arbour was behind the Islanders bench for 1,499 games with a 739–537–223 record.

Most games, career

2,141: Scotty Bowman, 1967–68 to 2001–02

One of Bowman's greatest qualities was his ability to stay so many steps ahead in a game and get the opportune matchups on the ice. He did it for more than 2,000 games.

Fewest games, career

1: Roger Crozier, Washington, 1981–82
2: Dick Duff, Toronto, 1979–80
2: Mike Rodden, Toronto, 1926–27
2: Godfrey Matheson, Chicago, 1932–33

Crozier's coaching career lasted one lonely game, a 3–1 loss to the Rangers on November 7, 1981, after he filled in on an interim basis between the firing of Gary Green and the hiring of Bryan Murray.

Most teams, career

8: Roger Neilson, 1977–78 to 2001–02

Neilson became titleholder of this unofficial record when he coached the Ottawa Senators in the two final regular-season games of 2001–02. The brief stint came courtesy of Ottawa coach Jacques Martin, who stepped aside so that Neilson could reach 1,000 games. Neilson also coached Toronto, Buffalo, Vancouver, Los Angeles, NY Rangers, Florida and Philadelphia.

7: Mike Keenan, 1984–85 to 2001–02

Keenan has been bench boss in Philadelphia, Chicago, NY Rangers, St. Louis, Vancouver, Boston and Florida.

Most "Original Six" teams coached

3: Dick Irvin, 1928–29 to 1955–56
3: Mike Keenan, 1984–85 to 2001–02
3: Pat Burns, 1988–89 to 2001–02

Irvin coached Chicago, Toronto and Montreal; Burns coached Montreal, Toronto and Boston; and Keenan coached Chicago, NY Rangers and Boston.

Most wins, career

1,244: Scotty Bowman, 1967–68 to 2001–02

Bowman has not only coached more games than anyone else, his 1,244 wins exceed the games-coached totals of all his peers except Al Arbour (1,606 games) and Dick Irvin (1,449 games). He is the only NHL bench boss to crack the 1,000-win mark.

Most wins with one team, career

739: Al Arbour, NY Islanders, 1973–74 to 1993–94

Arbour and his eyeglasses were twin institutions in Long Island.

Most losses, career

580: Scotty Bowman, 1967–68 to 2001–02
577: Al Arbour, 1970–71 to 1993–94

Considering the sheer quantity of games coached, Bowman should have owned this record long ago; but in fact, he only took the losses lead in 2001–02, his 30th NHL season.

Most losses with one team, career

537: Al Arbour, NY Islanders, 1973–74 to 1993–94
390: Jack Adams, Detroit, 1927–28 to 1946–47
360: Milt Schmidt, Boston, 1954–55 to 1965–66

Despite all the losses, Arbour only had five losing seasons with the Isles in 19 years behind the bench.

Most consecutive wins from start of career

6: Mario Tremblay, Montreal, 1995–96
5: Bep Guidolin, Boston, 1972–73
5: Marc Crawford, Quebec, 1994–95

Tremblay coached with the same enthusiasm that made him one of the top utility players on Montreal's championship teams of the 1970s. Unfortunately, that passion carried him only so far behind the bench. But he did have early success. His 40–27–10 record in 1995–96 included a six-game win streak from October 21 to October 31, 1995.

Most consecutive losses from start of career
8: Rick Paterson, Tampa Bay, 1997–98

Paterson is the only NHL coach to lose eight straight games from the start of his career. He was released without posting a single win, earning him further infamy: most consecutive losses by a winless coach.

Most minutes left in a game when a coach pulled his goalie for an extra attacker
18: Mike Keenan, Vancouver, November 25, 1998

Keenan pulled goalie Garth Snow with 18 minutes left in the third period of a game against Toronto, with Vancouver trailing 3–1 and on a power play. The attempt was unsuccessful. Keenan again pulled Snow midway through the period with the Canucks on another power play. This time, Leafs defenseman Dmitry Yushkevich scored into the empty net. Final score: Toronto 5, Vancouver 1. Keenan explained that he tried the gamble because he didn't think his team had the firepower to rally from behind.

Most goaltender changes by a coach, one game
9: Dick Irvin, Montreal, March 15, 1941

Coaches will try anything to find a winning formula. In the last game of a disastrous 16–26–6 season in 1940–41, Irvin alternated

Bert Gardiner and Paul Bibeault throughout the game. Gardiner was in action five times for 37 minutes and Bibeault four times for 23 minutes. Irvin switched his goalies at varying intervals from four to nine minutes. According to accounts of the day, Irvin felt his goalies came back into the play "mentally refreshed" from the pressures of the game. Bibeault said: "I was a little stiff when I went out there first each time," which led some to speculate that rinks "of the future" would be equipped with bullpens, "a small and separate ice surface to permit substitute players, particularly goalkeepers, to warm up while the game is in progress." The bizarre tactic worked: Montreal beat a weak NY Americans 6–0.

Highest winning percentage, career (min. 500 games)

.653: Scotty Bowman, 1967–68 to 2001–02
.634: Toe Blake, 1955–56 to 1967–68
.616: Glen Sather, 1979–80 to 1993–94
.612: Fred Shero, 1971–72 to 1980–81

Although he's the top dog in winning percentage, Bowman insists that his mentor, Blake, is the greatest coach of all time. He may be right or he may just be uncomfortable with the adulation.

Most games coached without making the playoffs

364: Red Sullivan, 1962–63 to 1974–75

In seven seasons behind the bench, Sullivan compiled a 107–198–59 record, an awful .375 winning percentage. None of his teams—NY Rangers, Pittsburgh or Washington—got close to the .500 mark.

Most games coached without winning the Stanley Cup

1,102: Billy Reay, 1957–58 to 1976–77

Reay was a fixture behind the Chicago bench from 1963–64 to 1976–77, winning several West Division titles with one of the era's highest-scoring teams. But Reay was dammed. He reached the finals three times and never won the Cup.

Shortest career by a Jack Adams Trophy winner (best coach)

164 games: Ted Nolan, Buffalo, 1995–96 to 1996–97

Unofficially blacklisted by old-guard management, Nolan hasn't been behind the bench since winning the coach of the year award in 1996–97. During that season he coached a no-frills Sabres team (on the back of Dominik Hasek) to a 40–30–12 record.

Most wins, one season

62: Scotty Bowman, Detroit, 1995–96
60: Scotty Bowman, Montreal, 1976–77

No one finds more ways to win than Bowman.

Fewest wins and most losses, one season (min. 70 games)

10 wins, 70 losses: Rick Bowness, Ottawa, 1992–93
11 wins, 71 losses: George Kingston, San Jose, 1992–93

Kingston and Bowness landed in impossible situations, coaching undermanned teams in a season in which scoring zoomed upward.

Fewest losses, one season (min. 70 games)

8: Scotty Bowman, Montreal, 1976–77
10: Scotty Bowman, Montreal, 1977–78
10: Scotty Bowman, Montreal, 1972–73
12: Pat Quinn, Philadelphia, 1979–80

Most wins by a rookie head coach (min. 70 games)
57: Tom Johnson, Boston, 1970–71
53: Mike Keenan, Philadelphia, 1984–85
53: Pat Burns, Montreal, 1988–89
Coaches are seldom handed the reins of the NHL's best team in their first season. But Johnson, the Bruins assistant general manager, got the plum assignment which came fully-loaded with all-stars Bobby Orr and Phil Esposito.

Fewest wins by a rookie head coach (min. 70 games)
13: Ebbie Goodfellow, Chicago, 1950–51
13: Frank Eddolls, Chicago, 1954–55
14: Curt Fraser, Atlanta, 1999–2000
16: Dave Chambers, Quebec, 1990–91
Goodfellow and Eddolls coached the Blackhawks during their darkest days, between 1946–47 and 1956–57, when the club finished last an astonishing nine times in 11 seasons in the six-team NHL.

Most losses by a rookie head coach (min. 70 games)
61: Curt Fraser, Atlanta, 1999–2000
58: George Kingston, San Jose, 1991–92
54: Steve Ludzik, Tampa Bay, 1999–2000
A rookie head coach on an expansion team: Is this a recipe for disaster? Fraser doesn't own the mark for fewest wins by a rookie coach (thanks to two Chicago coaches—see above) but he gets the nod for most losses after his disastrous 14–61–7 season. Yes, it was a bad idea.

Fewest losses by a rookie head coach (min. 70 games)

14: Tom Johnson, Boston, 1970–71

15: Toe Blake, Montreal, 1955–56

16: Joe Primeau, Toronto, 1950–51

16: Floyd Smith,* Buffalo, 1974–75

Johnson, holder of most rookie wins, beat out good coaches in outstanding years for this record. Blake and Primeau each won Stanley Cups in their rookie starts, while Smith (*a rookie with just one previous game in 1971–72) took Buffalo, in just its fifth NHL season, to the finals against Philadelphia.

Highest winning percentage, one season (min. 70 games)

.825: Scotty Bowman, Montreal, 1976–77

.806: Scotty Bowman, Montreal, 1977–78

.799: Scotty Bowman, Detroit, 1995–96

In Bowman's best season, the Canadiens lost only eight times for a 60–8–12 record.

Highest winning percentage by a head coach who coached a team for only one season

.667: Mike Keenan, NY Rangers, 1993–94

Keenan compiled a 52–24–8 record in 84 games.

Most teams coached, one season

2: Fred Glover, California and Los Angeles, 1971–72

2: Roger Neilson, Vancouver and Los Angeles, 1983–84

2: Ted Sator, NY Rangers and Buffalo, 1986–87

Neilson is the only one of these three recycled coaches that had to leave the state to take up his new post.

Most head coaches on one team, one season

3: several teams, including Tampa Bay, 1997–98

Terry Crisp coached Tampa Bay for 11 games, Rick Paterson for eight games and Jacques Demers for 63 games. The team ended the year at 17–55–10, finishing seventh in the Atlantic Division.

Most coaches hired who were also players for the team

17: NY Rangers, 1926–27 to 2001–02

For the first 50 years of its existence, until the hiring of John Ferguson as the franchise's 15th coach on January 7, 1976, New York had never employed a coach who didn't play for the club. Even the club's first coach, Lester Patrick, played a few games in Broadway blue. Since Ferguson, only two bench bosses—Fred Shero and Phil Esposito—have been former Rangers players.

Most new head coaches league-wide at start of season

10: 1997–98

Alain Vigneault (Montreal), Darryl Sutter (San Jose), Lindy Ruff (Buffalo), Ron Wilson (Washington), Pierre Page (Anaheim), Jim Schoenfeld (Phoenix), Kevin Constantine (Pittsburgh), Brian Sutter (Calgary), Pat Burns (Boston) and Wayne Cashman (Philadelphia).

CHAPTER 16

Chasing
Stanley

The quest for the Cup is always intense and brutal. It can also be capricious. Dale Hunter played 186 playoff games without winning the silver chalice. Henri Richard played 180 playoff games and captured it an all-time record of 11 times. Sadly, Richard still only owns one ring, his last from 1973. The others were stolen from his home.

Most times one person's name has been engraved on the Cup

17: Jean Béliveau, Montreal, 1953 to 1993

Although Béliveau won (only!) 10 Cups as a player, his name appears seven other times on the Cup between 1973 and 1993 as the Canadiens senior vice-president, a portfolio he assumed after his retirement in 1971.

Most Cups won by a player

11: Henri Richard, Montreal, 1956 to 1975

Richard will forever skate in the shadow of his famous brother, except when this record is hauled out.

Most Cups won by a player who is not in the Hall of Fame

9: Claude Provost, 1956 to 1970

Only three players—all Montreal Canadiens—have won more Cups than Provost. The bow-legged right-winger's main role with Montreal was shutting down the opponent's top left-wingers, which meant the likes of Bobby Hull, Frank Mahovlich and Ted Lindsay.

Most Cups won by a player who did not play for Montreal

8: Red Kelly, Detroit (4), Toronto (4), 1948 to 1967

In the 17 years from 1950 to 1967, Montreal copped eight Cups. Of the nine remaining Cups up for grabs, Kelly won eight of them. The only time he missed was in 1961, when Chicago won.

Most Cups won by a player with different teams (incl. non-NHL)

4: Jack Marshall, Winnipeg Victorias, 1901; Montreal AAA, 1902, 1903; Montreal Wanderers, 1907, 1910; and Toronto Blueshirts, 1914

4: Harry Holmes*, Toronto Blueshirts, 1914; Seattle Metropolitans, 1917; Toronto Arenas, 1918; and Victoria Cougars, 1925

*There is a debate whether the Blueshirts and Arenas should

count as one or two teams. Classified as one team, then Marshall stands alone.

Most Cups won by a player with different NHL teams

3: Gord Pettinger, NY Rangers, 1933; Detroit, 1936, 1937; and Boston, 1939

3: Al Arbour, Detroit, 1954; Chicago, 1961; and Toronto, 1962, 1964

3: Larry Hillman, Detroit, 1955; Toronto, 1964, 1967; and Montreal, 1969

3: Claude Lemieux, Montreal, 1986; New Jersey, 1995; and Colorado, 1996

3: Mike Keane, Montreal, 1993; Colorado, 1996; and Dallas, 1999

Pettinger and Arbour are the only NHL players to win three Cups without playing for Montreal.

Most names engraved on the Cup by one team

53: Detroit Red Wings, 1998

Of the record-setting 53 names that the 1998 Red Wings submitted for engraving on the Cup, only 26 were players.

Longest wait to win the Cup

21 years: Ray Bourque, Colorado, 2001

Bourque missed the playoffs only once in 22 seasons, but he didn't claim his first Cup until his last try with Colorado in 2001. It was his 214th playoff game.

Longest journey by a team to compete for the Cup

23 days: Dawson City Nuggets, 1905

The Nuggets' marathon cross-country trek covered 4,000 miles from Dawson City, Yukon, to Ottawa. They travelled by dogsled, foot, bicycle, boat and train, arriving just one day before their best-of-three finals series against Ottawa was set to begin. Ottawa refused to put back the start time and the exhausted Nuggets succumbed by scores of 9–2 and 23–2.

Most Cup celebrations in one city
41: Montreal, Quebec
In addition to the Montreal Canadiens' record 24 Stanley Cups, five other Montreal teams have won hockey's ultimate prize. The cast of champions includes the Victorias (5), the Wanderers (4), the AAAs (4), the Shamrocks (2) and the Maroons (2).

Smallest town to win the Cup
Kenora, Ontario, 1907
Kenora, a tiny railroad town located 140 miles east of Winnipeg, was no hub of commerce, but it did produce several excellent hockey teams in the early part of the 1900s. The Thistles, as the team was known, mounted failed Cup challenges in 1903 and 1905, before succeeding on its third attempt, downing the Montreal Wanderers 12–8 in a two-game total-goals series.

Largest TV audience for a playoff game
4.96 million: NY Rangers vs. Vancouver, June 14, 1994
Game 7 of this dramatic, fast-paced hockey series at Madison Square Garden drew a record number of television viewers, exceeding the 4.27 million that had watched the last game of the 1993 semifinal between Toronto and Los Angeles.

Most playoff games, career
240: Patrick Roy, Montreal, Colorado, 1986 to 2002
236: Mark Messier, Edmonton, NY Rangers, 1980 to 2002
231: Guy Carbonneau, Montreal, St. Louis, Dallas, 1983 to 2000
One of hockey's greatest playoff accomplishments belongs to

Roy, who took over this record in 2002, a goaltender leading all players in postseason games played. In fact, Roy has played more playoff games than anyone in the four major North American sports leagues.

Fewest games by a Cup winner, career
I: Gord Haidy, Detroit, 1950 semifinals
I: Doug McKay, Detroit, 1950 finals
I: Chris Hayes, Boston, 1972 semifinals
I: Steve Brule, New Jersey, 2000 conference finals

Four fortunate souls made their only NHL appearance during the play-offs for a Cup winner. Haidy and McKay were both called up by the Red Wings from the Indianapolis Capitols; Hayes by the Bruins from the Oklahoma City Blazers; and Brule by the Devils from the Albany River Rats.

Players who got their names on the Cup without playing any games for the championship team

Hal Winkler, Boston, 1929

Ted Green, Boston, 1970

Vladimir Konstantinov, Detroit, 1998

Winkler, who lost his Bruins' goaltending job to Tiny Thompson, and spent the 1928–29 season with the AHA Minnesota Milers, was listed as Boston's sub-goalie. Green's name was added at the Bruins' request although he had been sidelined for the entire season with a fractured skull. Konstantinov's career ended when he suffered serious head injuries in a car accident the previous spring. The defenseman's name was included as a tribute by the Red Wings.

Longest gap of years between Cups

15: Chris Chelios, Montreal, Detroit, 1986 to 2002

14: Mickey MacKay, Vancouver, Boston, 1915 to 1929

13: Craig Ludwig, Montreal, Dallas, 1986 to 1999

13: Brian Skrudland, Montreal, Dallas, 1986 to 1999

Number 13 was lucky for Ludwig and Skrudland, who reunited at Dallas' Reunion Arena to win it all.

Most Cup-winning teams captained

5: Jean Béliveau, Montreal, 1965, 1966, 1968, 1969, 1971

Béliveau captained Montreal for 10 seasons and won Cups in half of them.

Only player to captain Cup winners in different cities

Mark Messier, Edmonton, 1990; New York, 1994

Up to the 2001–02 season, Messier is the only player in NHL history to win the Cup while wearing the C for two different clubs.

Most playoff games without winning a Cup, career

186: Dale Hunter, 1981 to 1999

161: Brad Park, 1969 to 1985

160: Brian Propp, 1980 to 1994

Hunter reached the finals only once in his 19-year career: in 1998 with the Washington Capitals.

Most combined regular-season and playoff games without winning a Cup, career

1,593: Dale Hunter, 1981 to 1999

1,570: Dave Andreychuk, 1983 to 2002

Andreychuk is chasing down Hunter in the futility sweepstakes. Compared to Hunter's 1,407 regular-season and 186 playoff games, Andrechuk has a combination of 1,443 and 128 games.

Most Game 7s played, career

12: Glenn Anderson, 1981 to 1996
12: Patrick Roy, 1986 to 2002
11: Doug Gilmour, 1984 to 2002
11: Scott Stevens, 1983 to 2002

Anderson went to the wall six times with the Oilers, three times with the Leafs, twice with the Rangers and once with the Blues. He was on the winning side eight times. Fittingly, his last NHL game (with St. Louis in 1996), was a Game 7 tilt, a 1–0 double-overtime loss to Detroit in the conference semifinals. Roy played four with Montreal and eight with Colorado; winning six.

Only player to play every position in a playoff game

King Clancy, Ottawa, March 19, 1923

Clancy played forward and defense and even stepped between the pipes when goalie Clint Benedict left the ice to serve a two-minute penalty, as all netminders had to do when assessed a penalty in those days. Clancy's triple-duty came in Game 2 of the Senators best-of-three final series with the Vancouver Maroons.

Most family members' names engraved on the Cup, one playoff year

9: Ilitch family, Detroit Red Wings, 1997

In recent years, the practise of Cup-winning teams including consultants, accountants, public-relations flaks, masseuses, and towel boys on their rosters has reached epidemic propor-tions. When his team won the Cup in 1997, Red Wings owner Mike Ilitch took excess to a new level by listing himself and eight other members of his family as part of the champion-ship squad.

Only individual to win the Cup as an NHL player, coach and general manager
Jack Adams, 1918 to 1955

This might be hockey's rarest triple crown. Adams won the Cup twice as a player with the Toronto Arenas in 1918 and the Ottawa Senators in 1927; later as a coach and GM with Detroit in 1936, 1937 and 1943; and solely as a GM with the Red Wings in 1950, 1952, 1954 and 1955.

Age of the youngest player in the playoffs
17.3 years: Bep Guidolin, Boston, March 21, 1943

On December 9, 1942, Guidolin celebrated his 17th birthday playing left wing with the Bruins. He was the youngest NHLer ever. Three months later, he became the youngest playoff performer too.

Age of the oldest player to score in the playoffs
52 years: Gordie Howe, Hartford, April 9, 1980

Mr. Hockey scored his last NHL goal against Denis Herron in an 8–4 loss to Montreal in Game 2 of the 1980 preliminary round. Howe also picked up one assist in the three-game series.

Age of the oldest playoff scoring leader
36 years: Gordie Howe, Detroit, 1964

Howe never had a "best before" date throughout his career. He outlasted and outplayed all of his contemporaries, winning six postseason scoring titles, including his last in 1964 when he scored 19 points at age 36. Detroit lost to Toronto in the best-of-seven series 4–3.

Age of the youngest playoff goalie

18.7 years: Harry Lumley, Detroit, 1945

The Red Wings rookie lost his playoff debut 4–3 to Boston in the semifinals, but played superbly through the rest of the 1945 post-season, taking his club to within one game of the Cup.

Age of the oldest playoff goalie

44.5 years: Johnny Bower, Toronto, April 6, 1969

Bower went down with the ship. He lost 3–2 to Boston in Game 4 of the quarterfinals as the Bruins cuffed the Leafs aside in four straight.

Age of the youngest person to have his name engraved on the Cup

11 years: Stafford Smythe, Toronto, 1932

Smythe, the son of team owner Conn Smythe, was the Leafs' mascot.

Age of the youngest player to win the Cup
18.2 years: Larry Hillman, Detroit, April 14, 1955
18.10 years: Gaye Stewart, Toronto, April 18, 1942

Hillman and Stewart are among only a handful of teenagers to win the Stanley Cup. Another teenage champion is Pittsburgh's Jaromir Jagr, at 19.3 years, in 1991.

Age of the oldest player to win the Cup

42.9 years: Johnny Bower, Toronto, 1967

Bower was three months shy of turning 43 when the Leafs won the big prize in 1967. At least, that's what he claimed. Some contend he was actually a couple of years older than that.

Age of the youngest coach to win the Cup (since 1924)

30.8 years: Claude Ruel, Montreal, 1969
34.5 years: Cooney Weiland, Boston, 1939
34.8 years: Leo Dandurand, Montreal, 1924
35.3 years: Marc Crawford, Colorado, 1996

Ruel is rarely remembered today, and when he is, it's usually only as the pudgy guy who couldn't fill Toe Blake's shoes. But he managed an amazing feat in 1969: coaching Montreal to the Cup despite having no NHL experience and being younger than many of his players. Ruel got the chop in 1970.

Age of the oldest coach to win the Cup

68.9 years: Scotty Bowman, Detroit, 2002
60.8 years: Dick Irvin, Montreal, 1953
56.1 years: John Muckler, Edmonton, 1990

Bowman was eligible to collect social security when he won the Cup with the Red Wings in 1997, 1998 and 2002.

Average age of the oldest team to win the Cup

32.5 years: Detroit Red Wings, 2002
31.8 years: Toronto Maple Leafs, 1967

With eight players 35 or older, Detroit broke a 35-year record in 2002 by icing the league's oldest Cup champion. On average they were almost a year older than the famous Leafs' Over-The-Hill Gang of 1967.

Most octopi tossed onto the ice, one game

54: Detroit Red Wings, Joe Louis Arena, June 22, 1995

The peculiar postseason tradition of throwing octopi began in Detroit in 1952. It was meant to symbolize the eight playoff wins needed to claim the cup in those years. A record 54 octopi were hurled onto the playing surface during Game 3 of the 1995 Cup finals between the Red Wings and the New Jersey Devils. For those who are counting, 432 tentacles went splat at the Joe. The slimy onslaught failed to inspire the Wings, who went down in four straight games.

Largest octopus to hit the ice

50 pounds: Detroit, Joe Louis Arena, May 19, 1996

Bob Dubisky and Larry Shotwell, co-workers at a seafood company near Detroit, set the record by reaching the ice with a 50-pound octopus during Game 1 of the conference finals. Although this formidable feat received no air time on the nationally televised game, the monster mollusc was prominently displayed on the hood of the Zamboni between periods. The mystery remains however: How did they smuggle the creature into the arena?

Most rats tossed on the ice, one game

900: Florida, Miami Arena, June 8, 1996

Rats and the Florida Panthers became synonymous when winger Scott Mellanby killed one of the rodents with his hockey stick in the dressing room before the Panthers' home opener in 1995–96. After Mellanby scored two goals that night, goalie John Vanbiesbrouck told reporters that although Mellanby didn't get a hat trick, he did get a "rat trick." Rubber rats were tossed onto the ice every time Mellanby scored that season, but during the playoffs the ritual took a new turn as fans began hurling the vermin any time a Panther put the puck in the net. The rain of rats reached its crescendo after a Ray Sheppard goal in Game 3 of the 1996 finals, when some 900 fell from the heavens.

Most times the Cup was stolen during the playoffs

1: Chicago Stadium, April 1, 1962

Late in Game 3 of the 1962 semis between the Canadiens and the defending-champion Blackhawks, a Montreal fan named Ken Kilander broke the lock on the glass case housing the Cup in the Chicago Stadium lobby and began heading towards the door with the trophy. When an usher called out, "Hey, where are you going with that?' Kilander replied, "Back to Montreal where it belongs." Kilander didn't get far before he was tackled by police. He later claimed the caper was an April Fool's joke intended to get his picture in the paper.

Most hours a Cup-winning player wore his equipment
25: Shon Podein, Colorado, 2001

Podein kept his sweat-soaked duds on, skates and pads included, for 25 hours after the Avalanche won the Cup on June 9, 2001. The Colorado forward was provoked by a dare after he was told that a minor-league player in Adirondack had kept his equipment on for 24 hours. Podein spent a good portion of the 25 hours partying, before celebrating the end of his record-breaking stunt by jumping skates-first into a stream.

Most reported times the Cup was taken to a strip joint
2: in Edmonton, 1990; in New York, 1994

After winning his sixth Cup in 1990 with the Oilers, Mark Messier took the hallowed chalice to an Edmonton bar called the Forum Inn, set it on the stage, and let the girls gyrate on it. In 1994 with the Rangers, Messier repeated the stunt, taking Lord Stanley to Scores, Manhattan's most famous peeler palace, for some all-American loving. Said club spokesman Lonnie Hanover, "It was the first time I'd seen our customers eager to touch something besides our dancers."

Highest elevation the Cup has reached

14,433 feet: Colorado's Mt. Elbert, August 22, 2001

Each year, the individual members of the Cup-winning team get to spend 24 hours with the hallowed trophy. Mark Waggoner, vice president of finance for the corporation that owns the Colorado Avalanche, used his time to set a record. He led a climbing team that toted the 35-pound Cup to the top of Colorado's tallest peak on August 22, 2001. Aside from air travel, it is the highest elevation the trophy has ever reached. "I associated Mt. Elbert with what the Cup represents, being at the top, being the best," explained Waggoner.

Most stars awarded to one player, one game

3: Maurice Richard, Montreal, March 23, 1944

The Rocket whipped the Montreal Forum faithful into a frenzy by scoring all of his club's goals in a 5–1 win over the Leafs during Game 2 of the semifinals. Following the game, the public-address announcer stunned the crowd by stating, "Tonight's third star, from Montreal, No. 9, Maurice Richard!" As the crowd buzzed in puzzlement, he continued, "Tonight's second star, from Montreal, No. 9, Maurice Richard!" At this point understanding dawned and the applause began to build into a wild crescendo. "Tonight's first star, from Montreal, No. 9, Maurice Richard!"

CHAPTER 17

Sniper
alley

An ungodly number of playoff scoring records are held by the Edmonton Oilers. The top five all-time points leaders—Wayne Gretzky, Mark Messier, Jari Kurri, Glenn Anderson and Paul Coffey—all owe their lofty ranking to their years spent with the Oilers machine-gun offense of the mid-1980s. Edmonton was one of the few teams able to build a hockey dynasty without the foundation of an iron-clad defense.

Most goals by a player for one team, career

92: Jari Kurri, Edmonton, 1982 to 1990

85: Mike Bossy, NY Islanders, 1978 to 1987

It's not Wayne Gretzky or Mark Messier, but the Finnish-born Kurri that holds this mark. The first great Euro sniper, Kurri's shooting eye was always sharp in the postseason.

Largest differential goals to assists, career

38: Maurice Richard, 1943 to 1960

28: Dino Ciccarelli, 1981 to 1999

25: Reggie Leach, 1971 to 1983

25: Cam Neely, 1984 to 1996

Pure goal-scorer extraordinaire, the Rocket posted 82 goals against only 44 assists in 133 postseason games with the Canadiens. Ciccarelli is a surprising second with 73–45, followed by Leach with 47–22 and Neely with 57–32.

Most goals by a defenseman, career

59: Paul Coffey, 1981 to 2001

56: Denis Potvin, 1974 to 1988

Wayne Gretzky owns the all-time playoff mark with 122 goals. Among defensemen, the record total is halved by one-time Edmonton teammate Coffey, who broke Potvin's rearguard count in 1996 when he was with the Red Wings.

Most power-play goals by a defenseman, career

28: Denis Potvin, 1974 to 1988

26: Al MacInnis, 1982 to 2002

Defensemen still trail forwards for the all-time mark in this category—Brett Hull has 40 man-advantage goals—but not by much.

Most overtime goals by a defenseman, career

3: Ken Morrow, 1980 to 1989

Morrow didn't score many goals, but when he did they were often big ones. He scored his three OT goals against Los Angeles in 1980, Edmonton in 1981 and NY Rangers in 1984. The former NY Islander D-man has half the all-time record number of six OT goals owned by Maurice Richard, one of the Rocket's few remaining NHL marks.

Most power-play hat tricks, career

2: Dino Ciccarelli, Detroit, April 29, 1993, Game 6 of division semi-finals; May 11, 1995, Game 3 of conference quarterfinals

You'd never guess that Ciccarelli owns this unusual record. Even though he was only five-foot-ten and 185 pounds, the feisty winger scored most of his goals from the high-traffic areas in front of the net.

Most hat tricks by a defenseman, career

2: Paul Reinhart, Calgary, April 14, 1983, Game 1 of division finals; and April 8, 1984, Calgary, Game 4 of division semifinals

Reinhart was one of the most talented puck handlers to ever patrol an NHL blueline. Even so, he would still be a dark-horse candidate to hold this record.

Most assists by a defenseman, career

139: Ray Bourque, 1980 to 2001
137: Paul Coffey, 1981 to 2001

If it weren't for Wayne Gretzky and his all-time high 260 assists, this record might have been within striking distance by a defenseman. Mark Messier is second all-time with 186 assists followed by Bourque's 139. Bourque passed Coffey in 2001, his final postseason.

Most points by a defenseman, career
196: Paul Coffey, 1981 to 2001
180: Ray Bourque, 1980 to 2001
164: Denis Potvin, 1974 to 1988
Functioning like a fourth forward, Coffey averaged slightly more than a point per game throughout his playoff career. Top all-time mark is Wayne Gretzky's 382 points.

Most goals by a player who did not win the Cup, career
73: Dino Ciccarelli, 1981 to 1996
64: Brian Propp, 1980 to 1994
57: Cam Neely, 1984 to 1996
Ciccarelli is the surprise guest at this party for Cup rejects. Like Propp and Neely, he never found the right team at the right moment to win the Cup.

Most assists by a player who did not win a Cup, career
105: Adam Oates, 1986 to 2002
90: Brad Park, 1969 to 1985
It was as Brett Hull's centre that Oates achieved his greatest regular-season success, but he set up more postseason goals in Boston and Detroit than he did in St. Louis.

Most points by a player who did not win the Cup, career
148: Brian Propp, 1980 to 1994
143: Adam Oates, 1986 to 2002
Propp reached the finals with the Flyers in 1985 and 1987 and with the North Stars in 1991. He ranks second to Bobby Clarke on the list of Philadelphia's all-time playoff scoring leaders.

Most games without a goal, career

113: Craig Muni, 1982 to 1998

A forgotten defensive mainstay on the Oilers' Cup-winning squads of the 1980s, Muni won three Cups in Edmonton. Despite skating on six teams in 12 postseasons, including six with the high-flying Oilers, the Toronto-born blueliner never managed to put the puck in the net.

Most years leading all playoff scorers

6: Gordie Howe, Detroit, 1949, 1952, 1955, 1961, 1963, 1964

6: Wayne Gretzky, Edmonton, Los Angeles, 1983, 1984, 1985, 1987, 1988, 1993

Gretzky was 32 when he won his last playoff scoring title with the Kings in 1993. Howe copped three titles after age 32. He won his last in 1964, at age 36.

Most consecutive years leading all playoff scorers

3: Guy Lafleur, Montreal, 1977, 1978, 1979

3: Wayne Gretzky, Edmonton, 1983, 1984, 1985

Lafleur won the title outright in 1977 and shared the honour with teammates Larry Robinson in 1978 and Jacques Lemaire in 1979. Gretzky led the scoring parade with 38 points in 1983 even though the Oilers didn't win the Cup.

Most goals in three consecutive playoff years

51: Mike Bossy, NY Islanders, 1981, 1982, 1983

The Islanders gunner was so reliable it was scary. In three straight postseasons from 1981 to 1983, he scored exactly 17 goals each year.

Most even-strength goals, one playoff year

17: Reggie Leach, Philadelphia, 1976

16: Jari Kurri, Edmonton, 1985

Most people are aware that Kurri and Leach hold the mark for most goals in one playoff year with 19. What is not well-known is that both snipers compiled their record totals with virtually no help from the power play. Leach scored just two of his 19 goals with the man-advantage. Kurri scored only one of his 19 goals on the power play, but counted two others when the Oilers were shorthanded.

Most game-winning goals by a rookie, one playoff year

4: Claude Lemieux, Montreal, 1986

4: Chris Drury, Colorado, 1999

Who says rookies don't score clutch goals? Both of these young-sters were key contributors to their clubs' championship runs. Among veterans, the record of six game-winners is held by the two Joes: Joe Sakic in 1996 and Joe Nieuwendyk in 1999.

Most consecutive game-winning goals, one playoff year

4: Clark Gillies, NY Islanders, 1977, last game of preliminary round; and first three games of quarterfinals

More impressive than Mike Bossy's feat of four game-winners in one series (see page 175), Gillies nailed his four game-winners in a row.

Most four-goal games, one playoff year

2: Newsy Lalonde, Montreal, 1919

2: Wayne Gretzky, Edmonton, 1983

Lalonde scored five times against Ottawa goalie Clint Benedict in the first round and had a four-goal game in the Cup finals against Seattle's Harry Holmes. Gretzky burned Winnipeg's

Brian Hayward for four in the division semifinals and Calgary's Reggie Lemelin for another quartet in the division finals.

Most points by a player whose team did not reach the finals, one playoff year

35: Doug Gilmour, Toronto, 1993
33: Rick Middleton, Boston, 1983
32: Barry Pederson, Boston, 1983

Had these three played on better teams all of them would have had a shot at Gretzky's all-time postseason record of 47 points in 1984–85.

Most goals in a game by a player who was intoxicated
5: Reggie Leach, Philadelphia, May 6, 1976

Five NHLers own the record of five goals in a playoff game, but Leach is the only one of this elite club to do it while under the influence. Leach opted to take the Budweiser cure when he found himself unable to shake a horrific hangover before an afternoon playoff tilt against the Bruins in 1976. "Feeling loose," the Rifle then went out and rang up five in a 6–3 Flyers romp.

Most game-winning goals, one series

4: Mike Bossy, NY Islanders, 1983, conference finals

Bossy is the only shooter to wire four game-winners in one series. Even so, it was not quite so dramatic an achievement as it might seem. The closest margin in this high-scoring six-game series with Boston was three goals.

Most power-play goals by a defenseman, one series
5: Denis Potvin, NY Islanders, 1981, quarterfinals
Potvin anchored an extremely deadly Islanders power play. Considering he captained New York to four straight Cups, it's hard to fathom how Potvin didn't win the Conn Smythe Trophy. The all-time record of six power-play goals is held by Los Angeles' Chris Kontos, set during the 1989 divisional semifinals against Edmonton.

Most power-play goals by a defenseman, one game
3: Denis Potvin, NY Islanders, April 17, 1981, Game 2 of quarterfinals
The only D-man to score a power-play hat trick, Potvin recorded 28 of his 56 postseason goals with the man-advantage.

Most goals by a rookie, one game
4: Tony Hrkac, St. Louis, April 10, 1988, Game 4 of division semifinals
You have to wonder what possessed Hrkac that spring evening when he caught lightning in a bottle against Chicago. In 40 other postseason games he scored only three times. Five forwards share the all-time lead with five-goal games.

Most points by a rookie, one game
6: Mikko Leinonen, NY Rangers, April 8, 1982, Game 2 of division semifinals
A classic trivia stumper. The Finnish freshman had a hand in setting up six New York goals in a 7–3 win over Philadelphia. He recorded no other assists that postseason. The only other player to collect as many assists in a playoff game is Wayne Gretzky, who got six when the Oilers rocked the Kings 13–3 on April 9, 1987. The all-time mark among all players is eight points, owned by Patrik Sundstrom and Mario Lemieux.

Latest overtime goal

55:13 OT: Peter Klima, Edmonton, May 15, 1990, Game 1 of finals

Klima's overtime winner against Boston's Andy Moog sank the Bruins 3–2 and set the stage for an Oilers sweep.

Only rookie to lead all playoff scorers

Nels Stewart, Montreal Maroons, 1926, (6–3–9)

After a few years in the minors, Stewart joined the Maroons in 1925–26. He was an instant success, leading the NHL in goals and points in his rookie campaign. In the four games of the 1926 finals, Stewart notched six of his club's 10 goals as the Maroons captured the Cup.

Only player to score a playoff goal without playing a single regular-season game

Eddie Emberg, Montreal, March 29, 1945

Emberg was called up from the Quebec Aces for the 1945 semi-finals after he led the Aces in scoring in the Quebec Senior League playoffs. He saw action in two games and scored once in a 10–3 Montreal rout of the Leafs in Game 5. But Toronto won the series and Emberg went back into the minors, never to return.

Only player to score a playoff goal on a broken leg

Bobby Baun, Toronto, April 23, 1964, Game 6 of finals

Late in Game 6 against Detroit, Baun took a shot in the ankle and had to be removed from the ice on a stretcher. With his leg taped tightly and shot full of novocaine, he returned to score the winner on his first shift in overtime. The rugged defenseman played in Game 7 too and attended the Leafs' victory party before allowing doctors to put his damaged leg in a cast. Ever since there has been conjecture over what exactly was broken. In his 2000 biography, *Lowering the Boom*, Baun cleared up the mystery. He said it was a fracture of a small bone on the outside of his leg.

Most penalty minutes, career
729: Dale Hunter, 1981 to 1999
541: Chris Nilan, 1980 to 1992
519: Claude Lemieux, 1984 to 2002
Hunter was consistently chippy throughout his 19-year career. He played 186 games; Nilan, 111; and Lemieux, 226.

Most penalty minutes, one playoff year
141: Chris Nilan, Montreal, 1986
139: Dave Schultz, Philadelphia, 1974
124: Jay Miller, Boston, 1988
The Canadiens enforcer made a point of breaking Schultz's mark in the 1986 postseason with six weeks worth of snarly play. Like the Hammer, Nilan set his record for a Cup winner. Nilan notched his mark in 18 games, Schultz in 17 games and Miller in 12 games.

Most penalty minutes in last playoff game
38: Forbes Kennedy, Toronto, April 2, 1969
During Game 1 of the quarterfinals against Boston, Maple Leafs forward Forbes Kennedy played what turned out to be the last game of his career at the raucous Boston Garden. He made it a memorable exit, picking up four minors, two majors, a 10-minute misconduct and a game misconduct. The 150-pound Maritimer was one of the few Leafs to show much fighting spirit. The Bruins won the game 10–0.

Most penalty minutes, one game

42: Dave Schultz, Philadelphia, April 22, 1976

During Game 6 of the quarterfinals against Toronto, Schultz hammered away at the Maple Leafs, picking up one minor, two majors, one 10-minute misconduct and two game misconducts. While the Flyers tough guy was in the box, Toronto won 8–5.

Most penalties, one period

6: Ed Hospodar, NY Rangers, April 9, 1981

Hospodar collected two minors, one major, one 10-minute misconduct and two game misconducts to set this record in the first period of action in Game 2 of the preliminary round against Los Angeles. His angry eruption also established the most penalty minutes in one playoff period: 39.

Most playoff fighting majors, career

28: Chris Nilan, 1980 to 1992

21: Dave "Tiger" Williams, 1975 to 1998

Nilan's nickname was "Knuckles," which accurately describes his most important asset: stone fists. In 111 postseason games, the Boston-born bomber recorded 28 fighting majors, which is 20 more than his career playoff goal total.

CHAPTER 18

The Puck
stops here

Hockey observers didn't know what to make of Patrick Roy when he broke in with Montreal. He talked to his goalposts and resembled a Tourette's sufferer with his incessant twitching. Roy soon had opposing players talking to themselves. The 20-year-old backstopped the Habs to the Cup in 1986 and became the youngest player to win the Conn Smythe Trophy as playoff MVP.

Most Cups won by a goaltender

6: Jacques Plante, Montreal, 1953, 1956 to 1960
6: Ken Dryden, Montreal, 1971, 1973, 1976 to 1979

Dryden and Plante each won six Cups with the Canadiens in their first eight years. Dryden called it a career and retired at age 31, while Plante played another 10 seasons and hung up the pads at age 44.

Most playoff games for one team

132: Billy Smith, NY Islanders, 1973 to 1989

The proverbial money goalie, Billy the Axe chopped his way to 88 wins against only 36 defeats in postseason play with the Isles.

Most playoff games without winning the Cup

118: Curtis Joseph, 1990 to 2002
93: Ron Hextall, 1987 to 1999

Despite turning in several stellar playoff performances, Cujo has yet to reach the finals. He could go down in the books as the best netminder to never win the Cup.

Fewest regular-season games played by a goaltender who backstopped his team to the Cup

0: Earl Robertson, Detroit, 1937
6: Ken Dryden, Montreal, 1971

No netminder has won a Cup with less NHL experience than Robertson. The 26-year-old rookie was called up from the minors to replace injured starter Normie Smith in the 1937 play-offs. With Detroit trailing the Rangers two games to one in the best-of-five finals, he slammed the door on the Blueshirts, winning 1–0 and 3–0 to lead the Wings to the Cup. Oddly, Robertson never played a regular-season game for Detroit. Only a month after his playoff heroics he was dealt to the NY Americans.

Most Game 7s played by a goaltender, career
12: Patrick Roy, 1986 to 2002
St. Patrick has been through the fire of more Game 7s than any playoff netminder. He has been victorious six times, including one Game 7 triumph in the 2001 finals.

Best goals-against average, career (min. 35 games)
1.54: Lorne Chabot, 1927 to 1936, in 37 games
1.74: Dave Kerr, 1930–31 to 1940–41, in 40 games
1.88: Tiny Thompson, 1928–29 to 1939–40, in 44 games
Despite their stingy GAAs, Chabot and Kerr lost more playoff games than they won.

Highest career winning percentage, (min. 75 games)
.714: Ken Dryden, 1971 to 1979
.710: Billy Smith, 1973 to 1989
.663: Jacques Plante, 1953 to 1973
Smith saw his 88–36 record fall to Dryden (80–32) when he lost his last playoff decision to Washington in the 1986 division semifinals. Plante netted a 71–36 record.

Most minutes played, one playoff year
1,544: Kirk McLean, Vancouver, 1994
1,544: Ed Belfour, Dallas, 1999
Remarkably, both McLean and Belfour played exactly the same number of minutes, a highly unlikely occurrence when you factor in overtime. McLean's log with the Canucks in 1994 consisted of 24 games and nine overtime periods. Belfour performed in 23 games and 10 overtime periods for Dallas in 1999. The biggest difference? Belfour's team won the Cup.

Most games with one-or-fewer goals allowed, one playoff year

14: Martin Brodeur, New Jersey, 2000
13: Patrick Roy, Colorado, 2001
11: Dominik Hasek, Detroit, 2002

A team doesn't need much offense to win with this calibre of goaltending. Interestingly, the leaders all set their marks since 2000. Before 1999, the record was held by John Davidson, who compiled nine one-or-fewer goal games in 18 games with the Rangers in 1979.

Most playoff shutouts, career

22: Patrick Roy, Montreal (5), Colorado (17), 1986 to 2002
15: Clint Benedict, Ottawa (7), Montreal Maroons (8), 1919 to 1928
14: Jacques Plante, Montreal (10), St. Louis (4), 1953 to 1973

Roy's record total is largely a product of the glut of modern-day playoff games. Benedict posted his 15 goose eggs in 48 games in Cup competition (against both NHL teams and west coast clubs of the PCHA and WHL). Roy has played in 240 postseason games.

Longest shutout sequence, one playoff year
270:08: George Hainsworth, Montreal, 1930
248:35: Dave Kerr, NY Rangers, 1937
248:32: Normie Smith, Detroit, 1936

Hainsworth began his scoreless sequence for the Canadiens during a marathon four-overtime game in the 1930 semifinals against the Rangers and continued it into the second game of the finals versus Boston. Kerr's streak in 1937 extended over three series. Hainsworth's Habs won the Cup, but Kerr's Rangers came up short, losing to Detroit in the finals.

Longest overtime shutout

116:30: Normie Smith, Detroit, March 24, 1936

Smith stopped everything shot his way until Mud Bruneteau finally ended the drama by beating Montreal Maroons netminder Lorne Chabot at 16:30 of the sixth overtime period in Game 1 of the semifinals.

Longest overtime shutout sequence

162:56: Patrick Roy, Colorado, 1996 to 1997
160:15: Charlie Gardiner, Chicago, 1930 to 1934

Roy earned his overtime shutout run between Game 4 of the 1996 conference semifinals and Game 3 of the conference quarterfinals. A couple of minutes after Roy broke Gardiner's record, Chicago's Sergei Krivokrasov scored to end St. Patrick's shutout string.

Most wins, career

148: Patrick Roy, 1986 to 2002
92: Grant Fuhr, 1982 to 1999

It's all about winning in the playoffs and Roy's huge pile of Ws is impossible to ignore. You have to be very good for a very long time to reach this section of the stratosphere.

Most overtime wins, career

45: Patrick Roy, Montreal, Colorado, 1986 to 2002

The master of sudden death has lost only 15 of 60 career overtime playoff games, a winning percentage of .750.

Most overtime wins, one playoff year

10: Patrick Roy, Montreal, 1993

Roy was christened St. Patrick after performing miracles on St. Catherine Street. It is hard to imagine that any goalie will break this record.

Most consecutive wins, more than one playoff year

14: Tom Barrasso, Pittsburgh, 1992 to 1993

From Game 3 of 1992 division finals to Game 4 of 1993 division semifinals, Barrasso won 14 straight and scooped two Cups with the Penguins. Since then his career has taken a steadily downward trajectory.

Most consecutive overtime playoff defeats, career

7: Martin Brodeur, New Jersey, 1995 to 2000

After losing seven straight in sudden death (beginning with Game 3 of the 1995 conference finals), Brodeur might have had reason to fear extra time. If so, the Devils netminder didn't show it. He got the monkey off his back in fine style on June 10, 2000, blanking Dallas through 28:20 of OT in Game 6 of the finals, and capturing the Cup as the Devils prevailed 2–1.

Most shots faced, one playoff year

820: Kirk McLean, Vancouver, 1994, in 24 games
769: Ron Hextall, Philadelphia, 1987, in 26 games
740: Olaf Kolzig, Washington, 1998, in 21 games

McLean faced a load of frozen rubber in 1994. He stopped a record 761 shots and carried the underdog Canucks to within one game of the Promised Land.

Most shots faced by a Cup-winning goalie, one playoff year

709: Ken Dryden, Montreal, 1971, in 20 games
672: Bill Ranford, Edmonton, 1990, in 22 games

Dryden is the only goalie to handle more than 700 shots and win the Cup. Montreal played only three playoff series in 1971, so Dryden was clearly under siege. He was pelted with an average of 34.8 shots per game, a record high for Cup-winning goalies.

Highest save percentage, career (min. 1,500 shots)

.927: Dominik Hasek, 1991 to 2002, on 2,750 shots
.923: Johnny Bower, 1959 to 1969, on 2,374 shots
The Dominator rules the roost. Hasek's superior play finally resulted in his first Cup in 2002.

Highest save percentage, one playoff year

.978: Terry Sawchuk, Detroit, 1952, on 229 shots
.963: Bernie Parent, Philadelphia, 1968, on 214 shots
In what may have been the finest playoff goaltending display of all time, Sawchuk stopped 224 of 229 shots and logged four shutouts in eight games. No visiting player scored a goal at Detroit's Olympia during the 1952 postseason.

Most goals allowed, one playoff year

62: Felix Potvin, Toronto, 1993, in 21 games
61: Ken Dryden, Montreal, 1971, in 20 games
61: Pete Peeters, Boston, 1983, in 17 games
61: Jon Casey, Minnesota, 1991, in 23 games
Potvin didn't even make it to the finals. The Leafs laboured through three seven-game series and six overtime games before being eliminated by Los Angeles in the semifinals.

Most goals allowed by a goaltender who won the Cup

61: Ken Dryden, Montreal, 1971, in 20 games
59: Bill Ranford, Edmonton, 1990, in 22 games
Dryden, an untested rookie, had only played six NHL games before being tossed into the playoffs pressure-cooker. Even though his GAA was 3.00, he won the Conn Smythe Trophy as playoff MVP. Montreal would not have won the Cup in 1971 without his stellar play.

Most goals allowed, one series
38: Murray Bannerman, Chicago, 1985
Bannerman got sliced up by the Edmonton Oilers's offensive
buzzsaw. He surrendered his record total in five-and-half games
of work during the conference finals.

Most goals allowed, one game
11: Paul Bibeault, Toronto, March 30, 1944
Bibeault was on the receiving end of the worst defeat in playoff
annals as Montreal crushed the Leafs 11–0 in the concluding
game of the 1944 semifinals. Montreal owned Bibeault—literally,
he was Canadiens property. Midway through the 1943–44 season,
Montreal loaned him to the Leafs as a wartime replacement.

Fastest two playoff goals allowed
5 seconds: Glenn Hall, Chicago, April 11, 1965
If you blinked you might have missed it. Hall obviously did. During
Game 5 of the semifinals against Detroit, he was beaten at 17:35 and
17:40 of the second period by a pair of long shots off the stick of the
same player: Norm Ullman.

Most combined shots faced by opposing goalies, one game
207: Tiny Thompson, Boston and Lorne Chabot, Toronto,
April 3–4, 1933
When the red light flashed behind the Bruins net on a goal by
Toronto's Ken Doraty in the sixth period of overtime, it signalled
the end of the second-longest game in playoff history. Despite
battling for 164 minutes and 46 seconds, the two clubs scored
only one goal, due largely to the stellar goalkeeping of Thompson, who stopped 113 shots, and Chabot, who turned back 93.

Shots on net:

Thompson	12	20	11	8	19	12	15	14	3	114
Chabot	9	5	15	6	12	12	18	13	3	93

Most saves, one game

113: Tiny Thompson, Boston, April 3–4, 1933

Newspaper game accounts described the first two hours of action as fast-paced and offensive and praised Thompson for his brilliance. Even so, he lost the game and the series in the ninth period. All of the players must have been bone-tired at the finish. Four of the five games in this hard-fought semifinals between the Bruins and Leafs were settled in overtime.

Only goaltender to captain a Cup winner

Charlie Gardiner, Chicago, 1934

Gardiner and several other goalies were appointed captain in 1932–33 in response to a new NHL rule stipulating that a team captain had to be on the ice at all times. Gardiner won six of eight postseason games in 1934 and posted a 1.33 GAA. Two months after winning the Cup, he died of a brain haemorrhage. He was only 29.

Only goalie to win the Cup with a team that he didn't belong to

Joe Miller, NY Rangers, 1928

Miller, a rookie, was loaned to the NY Rangers by the NY Americans as an emergency replacement for injured starter Lorne Chabot. He played the last three games of the best-of-five 1928 finals, winning the last two, as the Rangers downed the Montreal Maroons. It was the only time in Miller's four-year career that he appeared in the postseason.

CHAPTER 19

The second
season

The NHL's second season is the only

season that truly matters, particu-

larly for the owners' and advertisers' bottom lines.

What it means for the players is a long war of attri-

tion. Forget those so-called reality TV shows, this is

the genuine *Survivor.* To claim the crown, a team

must win four best-of-seven series, each an

unscripted version of a wrestling cage match.

Most consecutive playoff appearances

29: Boston Bruins, 1968 to 1996

28: Chicago Blackhawks, 1970 to 1997

Making it to the postseason is an excuse for management to print money. The low-budget Bruins have earned a huge whack of cash for Boston's front office over three decades.

Most consecutive series won

19: NY Islanders, 1980 to 1984

This record looks more remote with each passing year. The Isles' record run was ended by Edmonton in the 1984 finals.

Most consecutive series won over one team

18: Montreal Canadiens, against Boston, 1943 to 1987

This storied rivalry was a bully act until 1988, when the Terry O'Reilly-coached Bruins finally snapped the Habs' secret spell.

Most playoff games by a team that has not won the Cup

291: St. Louis Blues, 1967 to 2002

Maybe it's time to start talking about a Blues curse. The drought in Missouri has reached 35 years.

Most playoff games by a team that failed to win the Cup, one year

26: Philadelphia Flyers, 1987

Mike Keenan's overachieving Flyers nearly gutted it out. Edmonton defeated his battle-weary squad in the seven-game finals.

Most playoff games by a team that did not make the finals, one playoff year

21: Toronto Maple Leafs, 1993
21: Colorado Avalanche, 2002

Winning three seven-game series is a daunting task. No team has managed it yet.

Most regular-season points by a team defeated in the first round

121: Boston Bruins, 1970–71
114: St. Louis Blues, 1999–2000

The first-place Bruins fell prey to the third-place Canadiens. The first-place Blues were eaten by the eighth-place Sharks.

Most consecutive years missing the playoffs

9: New Jersey Devils, 1979 to 1988
8: Washington Capitals, 1975 to 1982
8: Boston Bruins, 1960 to 1967

The New Jersey franchise's stretch of suffering included four years as the Colorado Rockies. The club qualified for the post-season only once its first 13 years in the NHL. The Capitals had to wait longer than any team to make the playoffs for the first time.

Most one-sided goal margin in a series sweep

20: Boston Bruins outscored St. Louis Blues, 28–8, 1972

The Bruins won by scores of 6–1, 10–2, 7–2 and 5–3 against the Blues in the semifinals.

Most one-sided goal margin in Game 7 of a series

7: Detroit Red Wings outscored Colorado Avalanche, 7–0,
June 1, 2002

After surviving two tough seven-game series earlier in the playoffs, the Avalanche may have simply run out of gas.

Whatever the reason, it was an embarrassing exit for the defending Cup champions and goalie Patrick Roy, who was pulled from the game after Detroit's sixth goal in the second period.

Largest regular-season points-spread between two opponents
60: Edmonton Oilers vs. Vancouver Canucks, 1986
In this Godzilla-Bambi matchup, the Wayne Gretzky-led Oilers (119 points) clashed with the Petri Skriko-led Canucks (59 points). The Oilers took the best-of-five division semifinals 7–3, 5–1 and 5–1.

Largest points-spread in a playoff upset
48: Los Angeles Kings defeated Edmonton Oilers, 1982
This upset is known as the Miracle on Manchester, after the street on which the L.A. Forum was located. Led by Wayne Gretzky— who rewrote the record book with a 92-goal, 212-point season—Edmonton became the first team in history to top the 400-goal plateau. But all that gaudy offense went to waste as the Oilers (111 points) were ambushed in the playoffs by the lowly Kings (63 points) in the best-of-five division semifinals 3–2. The Oilers, who allowed 27 goals in the five games, discovered that you need to play solid defense to win in the postseason.

Most former captains on a Cup winner
6: Dallas Stars, 1999
The list of former Cs in Big D included Mike Keane (Montreal), Guy Carbonneau (Montreal), Brett Hull (St. Louis), Joe Nieuwendyk (Calgary), Pat Verbeek (Hartford) and Brian Skrudland (Florida).

Most future NHL head coaches on a Cup winner
9: Detroit Red Wings, 1954
Clearly, several players on the 1954 Wings were watching coach

Tommy Ivan and taking notes: half the roster later became bench bosses. The players who later swapped uniforms for suits were Ted Lindsay, Alex Delvecchio, Marcel Pronovost, Red Kelly, Al Arbour, Vic Stasiuk, Bill Dineen, Johnny Wilson and Keith Allen. Arbour is the only one of the nine to win the Cup as a coach.

Most future Hall of Fame players on a Cup winner

11: Montreal Canadiens, 1973
10: Montreal Canadiens, 1956
10: Toronto Maple Leafs, 1967
This 1973 Canadiens squad was not part of either of Montreal's two great dynasties and so it is surprising to discover that it owns this record. The Hall of Fame came calling for Ken Dryden, Serge Savard, Larry Robinson, Guy Lapointe, Jacques Laperriere, Frank Mahovlich, Henri Richard, Yvan Cournoyer, Guy Lafleur, Steve Shutt and Jacques Lemaire.

Most rookies on a Cup winner

IO: Montreal Canadiens, 1986

The freshmen included Patrick Roy, Claude Lemieux, Stephane Richer, Brian Skrudland, Kjell Dahlin, Mike Lalor, John Kordic, David Maley, Steve Rooney and Randy Bucyk. Canadiens coach Jean Perron was a rookie too.

Most American-born players on a Cup winner

12: New Jersey Devils, 1995
The U.S. hockey system's finest moment: Neal Broten, Bob Carpenter, Bill Guerin, Shawn Chambers, Danton Cole, Tom Chorske, Kevin Dean, Jim Dowd, Chris McAlpine, Mike Peluso, Brian Rolston and Chris Terreri.

Most combined regular-season points of teams defeated in the playoffs by a Cup winner

405: NY Islanders, 1980, (Los Angeles, 74; Boston, 105; Buffalo, 110; Philadelphia, 116)

405: New Jersey Devils, 2000, (Florida, 98; Toronto, 100; Philadelphia, 105; Dallas, 102)

The Islanders' mark is the most impressive as it occurred before the league adopted a new system that rewarded one point for a regulation tie and two points for an overtime victory. The Isles, who had 91 points (the fifth-highest in the league), defeated three teams with more points. The Devils, who had 103 points (also the fourth-highest in the league), defeated one team with more points.

Worst regular-season winning percentage by a Cup winner

.385: Chicago Blackhawks, 1938

.475: Toronto Maple Leafs, 1949

This Blackhawks squad was the most unlikely Cup champion of all time. Chicago had eight American players, a Russian-born captain, Johnny Gottselig, and a former major-league baseball umpire, Bill Stewart, as their coach. And Cup favourites, they weren't, with a 14–25–9 record. Toronto had a 22–25–13 season.

Best regular-season winning percentage by a team that failed to win the Cup

.875: Boston Bruins, 1929–30

.800: Montreal Canadiens, 1944–45

The 1929–30 Bruins powerhouse (38–5–1) did not lose two games in a row all season until the finals. In the best-of-three finals, those two defeats cost them the Cup. Howie Morenz and the Canadiens won the best-of-three finals in two straight. Montreal (38–8–4) lost to Toronto 4–2 in best-of-seven semifinals.

Longest span of years without winning a Cup
54: NY Rangers, 1940 to 1994

The Rangers supposedly jinxed themselves when owner John Kilpatrick celebrated the club's 1940 championship by burning the paid-off arena mortgage certificate in the Cup. The curse was said to be protected by a dragon that lived under the ice at Madison Square Garden. In 1994, Mark Messier drew out his sword and slayed it.

First team to win the Cup without home-ice advantage in four series
New Jersey Devils, 1995

The Devils did it the hard way. Ironically, New Jersey had a shoddy 8–14–2 record on the road during the regular season.

Most losses by a Cup winner, one playoff year
8: Montreal Canadiens, 1971
8: Pittsburgh Penguins, 1991

Montreal had a 12–8 record. Pittsburgh was 16–8.

Most shots on goal, one game
114: Toronto Maple Leafs, April 3–4, 1933

Despite the record-setting barrage, the Leafs managed to score only once in a marathon six-overtime tilt with Boston. Once was enough, however, as Toronto prevailed 1–0 to take the semifinals series three games to two.

Fewest shots on goal, one game
6: Toronto Maple Leafs, May 8, 2000

Facing elimination in Game 6 of the conference finals, the Leafs directed a measly six shots (three in the first period, two in the second and one in the third) at New Jersey goalie Martin Brodeur in a 3–0 defeat. Several of Toronto's players blamed their miniscule total on the New Jersey shotkeeper. Others suggested it was because the Leafs were outclassed.

Fewest shots on goal by a winning team, one game
10: Chicago Blackhawks, April 13, 1974
10: New Jersey Devils, April 9, 1990
One shot was all it took for Chicago, who got a goal from Gaston Gingras 40 seconds into the first period against Los Angeles in Game 3 of the quarterfinals and then rode the air-tight goaltending of Tony Esposito to a 1–0 win. The Kings outshot the Blackhawks 33–10. In Game 3 of the 1990 divisional semifinals, solid netminding by New Jersey's Chris Terreri gave the Devils a 2–1 win against Washington, despite being outshot 21–10.

Most goals scored, one playoff year
98: Edmonton Oilers, 1985, in 18 games
95: Pittsburgh Penguins, 1991, in 24 games
94: Edmonton Oilers, 1984, in 19 games
No one could fill the net like the Oilers of the 1980s. Defying the maxim that defense wins championships, Edmonton played 18 games and averaged 5.4 goals per game in 1985.

Fewest goals by a winning team in a four-game sweep
10: Toronto Maple Leafs, 2001
The Leafs concentrated on defense, eking out a sweep against Ottawa by scores of 1–0, 3–0, 3–2 and 3–1 in the conference quarterfinals.

Fewest power-play goals allowed by a Cup-winning team, one playoff year (since 1967–68)
5: New Jersey Devils, 2000
The Devils allowed only five power-play goals in 63 opportunities, a 92.3 per cent kill rate. They did not give up a single power-play goal on home ice in 23 chances.

Fewest overtime games, one playoff year (since 1926)
0: 1963, in 16 games
There were only three one-goal games in the entire playoffs in 1963. In the semifinals, Toronto thumped Montreal in five, while Detroit topped the Hawks in six. In the finals, Toronto clipped the Wings in five.

Most overtime games, one series
5: Toronto Maple Leafs vs. Montreal Canadiens, 1951
Four games in the 1951 finals had the identical score: 3–2. The other was 2–1. Sid Smith, Ted Kennedy, Harry Watson and Bill Barilko netted the OT markers for Toronto. Maurice Richard scored the winner in Montreal's lone victory.

Most double-digit playoff shutouts suffered by one team
2: Toronto Maple Leafs, 1944 and 1969
Toronto lost 11–0 to Montreal on March 30, 1944, in Game 5 of the semifinals; and lost 10–0 to Boston on April 2, 1969, in Game 1 of the quarterfinals. These two humiliating defeats are not prominently featured in Toronto team histories.

Only franchise to win the Cup in a seventh-game overtime
Detroit Red Wings: 1950 and 1954
In more than eight decades of playoff action, only twice has a final series been decided with a Game 7 overtime. In both

cases, Detroit was the victor: against the Rangers in 1950 and Montreal in 1954.

Only playoff game delayed due to fog
Philadelphia Flyers vs. Buffalo Sabres, May 20, 1975
The stifling humidity in Buffalo's Memorial Auditorium during Game 3 of the finals created a low-lying fog bank that nearly caused the game to be cancelled due to impaired visibility. The eerie sight prompted Flyers goalie Bernie Parent to crack, "I wouldn't take my boat out in these conditions." Play was halted 12 times, as rink attendants skated in circles and waved towels to dissipate the mist.

Only playoff games never finished
Toronto Maple Leafs vs. Boston Bruins, March 31, 1951
Edmonton Oilers vs. Boston Bruins, May 24, 1988
The Leafs-Bruins tilt in Game 2 of the semifinals was suspended after one overtime period with the score deadlocked 1–1 because Toronto bylaws didn't allow a game to continue after midnight on a Saturday night. The Oilers-Bruins encounter in Game 4 of the finals was suspended during the second period after a power failure at Boston Garden. The final score was 3–3.

Most fines assessed prior to a playoff game
$24,000: Montreal and Philadelphia, May 14, 1987
In 1986–87, Montreal had developed a pregame ritual that consisted of either Claude Lemieux or Shayne Corson shooting the puck into the opposing team's empty net. After the pregame warmup of Game 6 in the conference finals with Philadelphia, Flyers tough guy Ed Hospodar and backup goalie Chico Resch attempted to stop the Montreal pair from scoring. A fight erupted and within seconds both teams had raced from their

dressing rooms and joined the melee. After the chaos was quelled, $24,000 in fines were levied.

Most penalty minutes, two teams, one game
298: Detroit Red Wings (152) vs. St. Louis Blues (146), April 12, 1991, Game 5 of the division semifinals

Fewest penalty minutes, two teams, one game
0: Toronto Maple Leafs vs. Detroit Red Wings, April 16, 1942
In the only penalty-free contest in playoff history, Toronto defeated Detroit 3–0 in Game 6 of the finals.

Fewest penalty minutes, one team, best-of-seven series
20: Detroit Red Wings, 1945
The Wings were assessed only 10 minors during the seven games against Toronto in the finals. The Leafs picked up eight minors, one major and the Cup.

Longest span a team had to play shorthanded, one game
20 minutes: Montreal Canadiens, April 10, 1947

Toronto took advantage of Maurice Richard's volcanic temper for two key goals in Game 2 of the finals. In the second period, the Habs' star grew so frustrated with his shadow Vic Lynn that he raked Lynn's scalp with his stick, earning a five-minute major. On the power play Toronto scored to make it 3–0. Later, the Rocket clipped Bill Ezinicki across the face. Richard received a 20-minute match penalty. In those days, a team had to serve the entire 20 minutes shorthanded. Toronto scored only once during its lengthy power play, but Richard was suspended for the series' next game.

CHAPTER 20

Bowed
but
unbroken

Coaching in the NHL is a tough and often thankless job. Coaches are paid less than their players and are the only team members who can get fired. In modern times, even winning a Cup is little guarantee of security. Just ask Ken Hitchcock, Larry Robinson and Marc Crawford, who were all gassed after guiding their teams to the winner's circle.

Most Stanley Cups

9: Scotty Bowman, Montreal (5), Pittsburgh (1), Detroit (3),
*   1967 to 2002*
8: Toe Blake, Montreal, 1955 to 1968

The gold standard. Of all of Blake's records, this is the one that
Bowman wanted most to eclipse.

Most years in playoffs

28: Scotty Bowman, 1967 to 2002
24: Dick Irvin, 1928 to 1956

Bowman has coached in more postseasons than Toe Blake and
Punch Imlach combined. His career began in St. Louis during
1967–68. The expansion team, heavily stocked with former
Canadiens, lost four one-goal games to Blake's mighty Habs.

Most teams coached in playoffs

5: Scotty Bowman, 1967 to 2002
5: Roger Neilson, 1977 to 2002

Bowman has claimed the Cup with three—Montreal,
Pittsburgh, Detroit—of the five teams he coached. He missed
with St. Louis and Buffalo. Neilson didn't win the silverware
with any of his five: Toronto, Buffalo, Vancouver, NY Rangers
and Philadelphia.

Most playoff wins, career

223: Scotty Bowman, 1967 to 2002
123: Al Arbour, 1970 to 1984
100: Dick Irvin, 1928 to 1956

Only two other coaches in NHL history have hit the century
mark in wins, while Bowman has surpassed 200. Arbour won his
games with St. Louis and NY Islanders; and Irvin won his in
Chicago, Toronto and Montreal.

Highest playoff winning percentage (min. 65 games)

.705: Glen Sather, 89–37–1, 1979 to 1994
.689: Toe Blake, 82–37, 1955 to 1968
.632: Scotty Bowman, 223–130, 1967 to 2002

Sather's impressive percentage is either a sign of his coaching genius or the excellence of the 1980s Oilers. Perhaps, it's a bit of both.

Most playoff losses, career

130: Scotty Bowman, 1967 to 2002
88: Dick Irvin, 1928 to 1956

Bowman has lost more playoff games than any other coach has won.

Most playoff games coached without winning a Cup, career

163: Pat Quinn, 1978 to 2002
120: Pat Burns, 1988 to 2002

Among his four teams—Philadelphia, Los Angeles, Vancouver and Toronto—Quinn reached the finals twice, one victory shy in 1994 with the Canucks and two wins short in 1980 with the Flyers.

Most playoff years coached without winning a Cup

13: Pat Quinn, 1978 to 2002
12: Billy Reay, 1957 to 1977
11: Emile Francis, 1965 to 1983
11: Roger Neilson, 1977 to 2002

Quinn has never had trouble getting his teams into the playoffs; he just has never found one that could go the distance.

Most playoff wins by a rookie coach

15: Jean Perron, Montreal, 1986
12: Claude Ruel, Montreal, 1969
12: Al MacNeil, Montreal, 1971

Montreal has enjoyed more success with rookie coaches than any other franchise. All three of these first-year wonders won the Cup. A fourth Montreal rookie coach, Toe Blake, won the Cup in his first year behind the bench in 1956.

Fewest regular-season wins by a Cup-winning coach

4: Larry Robinson, New Jersey, 1999–2000

Championship-bound teams don't often change horses in midstream, but New Jersey did in 1999–2000, bringing in the Big Bird to replace Robbie Ftorek after 74 regular-season games.

Most points scored by a coach in the playoffs

1: Doug Harvey, NY Rangers, 1962
1: Charlie Burns, Minnesota, 1970

Harvey and Burns are not the only playing-coaches to suit up in the postseason, but they are the only ones who got their names on the scoresheet. Burns, who played 50 regular-season and six playoff games with the North Stars, recorded one goal in the 1970 postseason. Harvey, who skated in 69 regular-season games and six playoff games for the Rangers, recorded one assist in the 1962 postseason.

Only coach to make an appearance in the nets in the playoffs

Lester Patrick, NY Rangers, 1928, Game 2 of finals

Only in hockey could a 44-year-old coach who had never played goal before strap on the bloody pads of a fallen goaltender and win a game in the finals in overtime. On April 7, 1928, after Rangers netminder Lorne Chabot was carried out unconscious,

Patrick stepped into the breach and stopped all but one shot through two periods and a sudden-death overtime.

Only coaches who won the Jack Adams Award and the Cup in the same year

Fred Shero, Philadelphia, 1974
Scotty Bowman, Montreal, 1977

The Jack Adams Award, honouring the NHL's outstanding coach of the regular season, has been handed out since 1974. According to the voters, only twice in those 28 years has the year's best coach succeeded in winning the Cup: Shero in 1974 and Bowman in 1977. Typically, Adams and Stanley don't mix: Glen Sather, who coached Edmonton to four Cups in five years, won the award in 1986, the one year in that string that the Oilers were bounced out of the playoffs. Al Arbour, who piloted the NY Islanders to four straight Cups from 1980 to 1984, won the Adams in 1979, a year in which the Isles were ousted in the quarterfinals.

CHAPTER 21

The
last dance

Unlike many NHL records that are dominated by the Gretzkys and Roys, standards from the Stanley Cup final series still belong to hockey's old-time heroes. Time has forgotten the finals record book. Maurice Richard leads all goals scorers; Red Kelly has the most games; Jacques Plante owns the most wins; and Gordie Howe amassed the most penalty minutes.

Most games, career

65: Red Kelly, Detroit (37), Toronto (28), 1948 to 1967
65: Henri Richard, Montreal, 1956 to 1975
64: Jean Béliveau, Montreal, 1951 to 1971

It's amazing that a player who never wore the Canadiens colours could share top billing in this category. Success just seemed to follow Kelly around.

Most game-winning goals, career

9: Jean Béliveau, 1951 to 1971
8: Maurice Richard, 1943 to 1960
6: Bernie Geoffrion, 1951 to 1968
6: Yvan Cournoyer, 1964 to 1979

All these guys were French-Canadian and all of them did their scoring for Montreal.

Most goals in a Cup-clinching game

4: Babe Dye, Toronto St. Pats, March 28, 1922, against Vancouver Millionaires

Dye scored four of Toronto's five goals in a 5–1 victory. This is the playoffs' longest-surviving scoring record.

Fewest goals by a player who scored a Cup-winning goal, career

6: Gizzy Hart, Victoria Cougars, 1925
22: Pete Langelle, Toronto, 1942
26: Bill Barilko, Toronto, 1951

Gizzy's real name was Wilfred. He notched the game-winner in the Cougars 6–1 victory over the Canadiens in the 1925 finals. Hart played for three seasons in the Pacific Coast Hockey Association, then three years in the NHL after the PCHA folded in 1927.

Fastest Cup-winning goal
0:14: Jean Béliveau, Montreal, May 1, 1965, Game 7 of finals against Chicago's Glenn Hall

Béliveau didn't wait long to put his team on the board. His goal on the game's first shift stood up as the winner in a 4–0 Montreal shutout. The Habs' captain collected 16 points in 13 postseason games in 1965 and won the Conn Smythe Trophy.

Latest Cup-winning goal
54:51 OT: Brett Hull, Dallas, June 19, 1999, Game 6 against Buffalo's Dominik Hasek

The longest Cup-deciding game in history ended with a goal that should not have counted. Hull was in the crease when he potted the clincher. Final score: 2–1.

Only players to score Cup winners in their last game
Carl Voss, Chicago, April 12, 1938
Pete Langelle, Toronto, April 18, 1942
Bill Barilko, Toronto, April 21, 1951
Jacques Lemaire, Montreal, May 21, 1979

Voss scored his Cup winner in a 4–1 triumph over Toronto in Game 4 of the 1938 finals. A knee injury in training camp the next fall ended his career. Langelle potted his in a 3–1 victory over Detroit in Game 7 of the 1942 finals, capping off the greatest comeback in finals history, as the Leafs rallied to win four straight games to take the Cup. Langelle's career ended shortly afterward when he joined the war effort as part of the Royal Canadian Air Force. Barilko's OT winner deep-sixed Montreal in Game 5 of the 1951 finals. He perished in a plane crash four months later. Lemaire got his winner and retired in 1979 with eight Cups.

Only player to score a Cup-winning goal and be accused of being a Russian spy
Bill Barilko, Toronto, 1951

Four months after scoring the Cup-clincher in the 1951 playoffs, the Leaf hero flew north from his hometown of Timmins, Ontario, on a fishing trip and was never seen again. Barilko's vanishing act sparked bizarre rumours; it was even suggested in the newspapers that he was a Russian spy who had defected over the North Pole back to his ancestral homeland. It wasn't until 11 years later, in 1962, that the mystery was solved when Barilko's skeleton was found amid the wreckage of his plane in northern Ontario.

Only players to score Cup-winning goals in consecutive years

Jack Darragh, Ottawa, 1920 and 1921
Mike Bossy, NY Islanders, 1982 and 1983

Darragh's feat is long forgotten. Just two years after scoring his second Cup-winner, his career came to a sudden and tragic end when he died of a ruptured appendix at age 34.

Only players to score overtime Cup-winning goals in a Game 7

Pete Babando, Detroit, April 23, 1950, against NY Rangers'
    Chuck Rayner
Tony Leswick, Detroit, April 16, 1954, against Montreal's
    Gerry McNeil

It's only been done twice and both times by Red Wings. Neither Babando or Leswick would be a likely choice for the honour. The two left-wingers both scored only six regular-season goals the year they entered the history books.

Only brothers to score Cup-winning goals

Corbett and Cy Denneny: Corbett with Toronto Arenas in 1917,
Cy with Ottawa in 1927
Maurice and Henri Richard: Maurice with Montreal in 1956,
Henri with Montreal in 1966 and 1971

The Dennenys never played on the same team. The Richards played together for five seasons in Montreal and won the Cup each time.

Only defenseman to score two Cup-winning goals

Bobby Orr, Boston, 1970 and 1972

The incomparable No. 4 notched his first Cup winner in overtime to give the Bruins a 4–3 victory over St. Louis in 1970. He scored his second in a 3–0 win over the Rangers in Game 6 of the 1972 finals.

Age of the youngest player to score a Cup-winning goal

21.4: Ted Kennedy, Toronto, April 19, 1947, Game 6 of finals against Montreal's Bill Durnan

Despite his youth, Kennedy was already in his fourth full season and a proven club leader when he scored his 1947 Cup winner to make it 2–1 for Toronto.

Age of the oldest player to score a Cup-winning goal

36.5: Bill Cook, NY Rangers, 1933, against Toronto's Lorne Chabot

The Rangers captain capped off a year in which he also won the scoring title by notching the 1933 Cup winner at 7:34 of overtime. The game ended 1–0.

Age of the oldest player to score in finals

41.6 years: Igor Larionov, Detroit, June 10, 2002

Larionov scored twice against Carolina in the 2002 finals. His first goal (June 8) ended a triple-overtime marathon in Game 3. Not bad for the oldest guy on the ice.

Most finals games without scoring a goal, career

24: Gerry Melnyk, 1956 to 1968
24: Craig MacTavish, 1980 to 1997

Surprisingly this record does not belong to a defenseman. Both of these players were centres. Melnyk played in five finals with Detroit, Chicago and St. Louis without turning on the red light. MacTavish played in four finals, three with Edmonton and one with the NY Rangers, without finding the net.

Most finals games without scoring a point, career

24: Gerry Melnyk, 1956 to 1968

Melnyk picked up 12 points in 29 other playoff games, but oddly not a single point in 24 games in the finals.

Most overtime goals, career

3: Maurice Richard, Montreal, 1942–43 to 1959–60

The ever-dangerous Rocket came through in sudden death in 1946, 1951 and 1958.

Most overtime points, career

4: Maurice Richard, Montreal, 1942–43 to 1959–60

Richard was always the go-to-guy for Montreal when the game was on the line. His total is comprised of three goals and one assist.

Most overtime goals, one series

2: Don Raleigh, NY Rangers, 1950
2: John LeClair, Montreal, 1993

Raleigh and LeClair both nailed their overtime winners in back-to-back games. Raleigh did it in Games 4 and 5 of a seven-game series against Detroit; LeClair did it in Games 3 and 4 of a five-game series against Los Angeles.

Fastest overtime goal
0:09: Brian Skrudland, Montreal, May 18, 1986, Game 2 against Calgary
0:31: Buzz Boll, Toronto, April 9, 1936, Game 1 against Detroit
Some fans hadn't made it back from the washrooms when Skrudland beat goalie Mike Vernon to end this 1986 tilt.

Most goals by a defenseman, career
8: Bobby Orr, Boston, in 16 games
8: Denis Potvin, NY Islanders, in 24 games
8: Paul Coffey, Edmonton (7), Detroit (1), in 32 games
If Orr's knees hadn't disintegrated, he'd probably own this record outright.

Most points by a defenseman, career
33: Doug Harvey, 1948 to 1969, in 50 games
26: Denis Potvin, 1974 to 1988, in 24 games
26: Paul Coffey, 1981 to 2001, in 32 games
Another significant record that is not listed anywhere. Harvey counted four goals and 29 assists. He recorded 32 points with Montreal and one with St. Louis. It's worth noting that Harvey played in 27 more finals games than Potvin and 18 more than Coffey.

Most goals by a defenseman, series
5: Denis Potvin, NY Islanders, 1980, in 6 games
5: Al MacInnis, Calgary, 1989, in 6 games
5: Brian Leetch, NY Rangers, 1994, in 7 games

Most goals by a defenseman, one game
3: Eric Desjardins, Montreal, June 3, 1993, Game 2 against Los Angeles
Desjardins is the only D-man to notch a hat trick in the finals.

Most points by a defenseman, one game
5: Eddie Bush, Detroit, (1–4), April 9, 1942, against Toronto in Game 3 of finals
Bush is one of the most obscure playoffs record-holder. He spent the majority of his career in the minors and made only one NHL postseason appearance. He had a hand in all five Red Wings goals in a 5–2 win over the Leafs in the 1942 finals.

Most goals by a rookie, series
6: Nels Stewart, Montreal Maroons, 1926, in 4 games
5: Roy Conacher, Boston, 1939, in 5 games
Official record books mysteriously deny Stewart this record. He certainly didn't play like a rookie in the 1926 postseason. He scored six out of the 10 goals the Maroons notched against the Victoria Cougars and he was the only player in the finals to post more than three points.

Most points by a rookie, series
7: Nels Stewart, Montreal Maroons, 1926, in 4 games
7: Roy Conacher, Boston, 1939, in 5 games
7: Ralph Backstrom, Montreal, 1959, in 5 games
Backstrom is the only one of these three who didn't go on to become a top sniper. He recorded seven of his eight postseason points in 1959 in the finals.

Most penalty minutes in the finals, career

94: Gordie Howe, Detroit, in 55 games

87: Kevin McClelland, Edmonton, in 22 games

86: Duane Sutter, NY Islanders, in 24 games

This is one of the few playoff records owned by Howe that Gretzky didn't erase.

Highest winning percentage by a goalie, career (min. 15 games)

.750: Ken Dryden, Montreal, 1971 to 1979

.739: Billy Smith, NY Islanders, 1973 to 1989

.737: Grant Fuhr, Edmonton, 1984 to 1988

As the cage custodian of a Montreal dynasty, Dryden never lost a finals series. He netted a 24–8 record, Smith 17–6 and Fuhr 14–5.

Lowest goals-against average, career (min. 15 games)

1.55: Clint Benedict, Ottawa, Montreal Maroons, 1918 to 1930

1.82: Gump Worsley, Montreal, 1953 to 1974

1.86: Gerry McNeil, Montreal, 1948 to 1957

1.88: Patrick Roy, Montreal, Colorado 1986 to 2002

A good chunk of Benedict's career overlapped with the lowest scoring era in hockey history. Worsley's career was rejuvenated when he was traded from the Rangers to Montreal in June 1963.

Most shutouts, career

8: Clint Benedict, Ottawa (4), Montreal Maroons (4),
  1918 to 1930

4: Turk Broda, Toronto, 1937 to 1952

4: Jacques Plante, Montreal, 1953 to 1973

4: Patrick Roy, Montreal (1), Colorado (3), 1986 to 2002

Benedict, who won three Cups with Ottawa and one with the Maroons, has a stranglehold on this record.

Most shutouts, one series

3: Clint Benedict, Montreal Maroons, 1926

3: Frank McCool, Toronto, 1945

In more than 80 years, only two netminders have recorded three zeroes in a finals. Benedict got his in four games, McCool in seven.

Most consecutive shutouts, one series
3: Frank McCool, Toronto, 1945

The Leafs' rookie puck stopper blanked Detroit in the first three games of the 1945 finals by scores of 1–0, 2–0 and 1–0.

Longest shutout sequence, more than one year

229:22: Clint Benedict, 1923 to 1926

227:41: Patrick Roy, Colorado, 1996 to 2001

193:39: Terry Sawchuk, Detroit, 1952 to 1954

Roy fell just short of Benedict's 77-year record after beating Florida 1–0 in the third overtime period during the last game of the 1996 finals, and winning the first game of the 2001 finals 5–0 against Dallas.

Longest shutout sequence, one series

188:35: Frank McCool, Toronto, 1945

161:23: Terry Sawchuk, Detroit, 1952

No rookie has played any better than McCool did in 1945. After stoning the first-place Canadiens in the semis, he blanked the Red Wings in the first three games of the finals. Detroit battled back to even the series, before McCool and the Leafs eked out a 2–1 victory in Game 7 on hostile Olympia ice.

Most minutes played by a goalie, career

2,423: Jacques Plante, Montreal, St. Louis, 1953 to 1970
2,369: Turk Broda, Toronto, 1937 to 1952
2,185: Terry Sawchuk, Detroit, Toronto, 1950 to 1970

Plante played a record 41 games in the finals, including 2,279 minutes in Montreal. His minute totals only surpassed Broda in 1969 and 1970 when Plante was with the expansion Blues (164 minutes).

Most minutes played by a goalie, one series

459: Harry Lumley, Detroit, 1950
459: Chuck Rayner, NY Rangers, 1950

The 1950 Wings-Rangers series was a classic roller-coaster seven-game series with three sudden-death games, including Game 7's double-overtime thriller.

Fewest goals allowed, one series (since 1939)

2: Terry Sawchuk, Detroit, 1952

Uke didn't allow Montreal to score more than one goal in any of the four games of the Detroit sweep.

Most goals allowed, one series

32: Tony Esposito, Chicago, 1973
25: Johnny Mowers, Detroit, 1942

Esposito lost to Montreal in both of his trips to the finals with the Blackhawks. His GAA was 5.33 in the 1973 six-game tilt.

Most goals allowed, one game

9: George Hainsworth, Toronto, April 7, 1936
9: Johnny Mowers, Detroit, April 14, 1942

Both of these drubbings occurred in an era when the goalie

was expected to play the entire 60 minutes, regardless of the score. Hainsworth lost 9–4 against Detroit; and Mowers 9–3 against Toronto.

Most goals allowed by two opposing goalies, one game
15: Ken Dryden, Montreal and Tony Esposito, Chicago, May 8, 1973
It's hard to believe that these were the same two goalkeepers who held the fort for Canada at the 1972 Summit Series. Final score: Chicago 8–Montreal 7.

Only goalie to allow two Cup-winning goals in overtime
Gerry McNeil, Montreal, 1951 and 1954
McNeil's misfortunes in Game 7s—scored on by Toronto's Bill Barilko in 1951 and Detroit's Tony Leswick in 1954—contributed to him being replaced by Jacques Plante in 1955.

Most finals lost by a coach
12: Dick Irvin, Chicago (1), Toronto (6), Montreal (5), 1928 to 1956
Irvin has absolutely no competition in this category.

Most losses by a coach in the finals
45: Dick Irvin, Chicago (3), Toronto (20), Montreal (22),
      1928 to 1956
22: Scotty Bowman, St. Louis (12), Montreal (5), Detroit (5),
      1967 to 2002
16: Punch Imlach, Toronto, 1958 to 1980
The number next to Irvin's name belongs in another era. No coach in today's game would ever survive winning only four of the 16 finals he coached in.

Best winning percentage by a coach (min. 12 games)

.714: Hap Day, Toronto, 1940 to 1950

.708: Toe Blake, Montreal, 1955 to 1968

.708: Al Arbour, NY Islanders 1970 to 1994

It's unfortunate that none of these three masterminds ever matched wits in the playoffs. Day recorded a 20–8 record; Blake was 34–14; and Arbour was 17–7.

Worst winning percentage by a coach (min. 12 games)

.333: Sid Abel, Detroit, 1952 to 1976

.333: Lester Patrick, NY Rangers, 1926 to 1939

.347: Mike Keenan, Philadelphia, Chicago, NY Rangers, 1984 to 2002

Abel is the only coach to reach the finals four times and lose each time. He had more luck in the finals as a player, winning three Cups with Detroit. Abel notched an 8–16 record; Patrick was 5–10; and Keenan was 8–15.

Most Cups by a team (since 1893)

24: Montreal Canadiens, 1910 to 2002

Montreal has captured 24 Stanley Cups, a record that could well last forever even if the Habs never win another one. The Toronto Maple Leafs, at 13, are a distant second and are not closing any ground, having last won the Cup in 1967. Between them, these two tradition-soaked Canadian clubs have won more Cups than all of the American teams combined.

Most home games in the finals that a team played on the road because of the circus

11: New York Rangers, 1928 to 1950

Scheduling conflicts with the Barnum & Bailey Circus likely cost the Rangers a couple of Cups. In six of the seven finals the Rangers appeared in from 1928 to 1950, the club was forced to vacate Madison Square Garden for the clowns and elephants. This meant they had to play 11 of 16 home games on the road, at either their opponent's arena or at a neutral site. It wasn't until 1994 that New York fans finally got to see their team win the Cup on home ice.

Largest point-differential between two finalists

41: NY Islanders (118 points) vs. Vancouver, 1982 (77 points)
34: Montreal (83 points) vs. Chicago, 1944 (49 points)
This looked like a massacre in the making, but the feisty Canucks refused to roll over. Although the Islanders took the series in four straight, all the games were closely contested.

Most consecutive wins in the finals

10: Montreal Canadiens, May 9, 1976 to May 18, 1978
10: Toronto Maple Leafs, April 19, 1947 to April 11, 1951
Beginning with a four-game sweep of the defending-champion Flyers in 1976, the Canadiens reeled off 10 straight wins before finally losing 4–0 to Boston in Game 3 of the 1978 finals. Although it was not accomplished in consecutive years, Toronto also won 10 straight games in the finals. The Leafs' streak was broken in overtime by Montreal in Game 2 of the 1951 finals. Toronto won that series in five games. If not for that lone defeat, the blue and white would have chalked up 13 straight victories.

Most overtime wins, one team, one series

4: Toronto Maple Leafs, 1951
Toronto beat Montreal 4–1 in the series by scores of 3–2, 2–1, 3–2 and 3–2. The second game, Montreal's only win, was also in overtime. The 1951 Toronto-Montreal series is also the only finals round in which every game ended in overtime.

Largest winning margin in a Cup-clinching game

8 goals: Pittsburgh defeated Minnesota 8–0, May 25, 1991

Blowouts are rare when the Cup is up for grabs, but in the 1991 finals, Mario Lemieux and the Penguins embarrassed the North Stars at the Met Center in Game 6 of the finals, rolling to an 8–0 whitewash.

Latest date of a finals game

June 24, 1995: New Jersey Devils vs. Detroit Red Wings

The Devils bagged the Cup in four straight games with a 5–2 win over the Red Wings. For the first and only time the game of winter ended its season in summer.

ACKNOWLEDGEMENTS

Thanks to the following for the use of statistical material:

- *The Official* NHL *Guide and Record Book,* various years
- *Total Hockey* and *Total Stanley Cup*
- *The Trail of the Stanley Cup* by Charles H. Coleman
- NHL *Team Guides,* various years
- *The Hockey Trivia* series and *Old-Time Hockey Trivia* series by Don Weekes
- *Pavel Bure: The Riddle of the Russian Rocket* by Kerry Banks
- *The Rules of Hockey* by James Duplacey
- *The Hockey Compendium* by Jeff Klein and Karl-Eric Reif
- ESPN *Did You Know*
- *What's the Score* by Liam McGuire
- *Hockey Hall of Fame,* edited by Dan Diamond
- *The Hockey News Century of Hockey,* edited by Steve Dryden
- *Stats Hockey Handbook*
- Also, *The Hockey News, hockeydb.com, faceoff.com, Sports Illustrated, The Sporting News, National Post, Globe and Mail, Vancouver Sun,* and *Montreal Gazette.*

Thanks to the following for use of quoted material:

From *The Stick: A History, A Celebration, an Elegy,* by Bruce Dowbiggin. Published by Macfarlane, Walter & Ross.

The authors gratefully acknowledge the help of everyone at *The Hockey News;* Gary Meagher and Benny Ercolani of the NHL; Phil Pritchard at the Hockey Hall of Fame; the staff at the McLellan-Redpath Library at McGill University; Rob Sanders, Susan Rana and Chris Labonte at Greystone Books; the many hockey writers, broadcast-journalists, media and Internet organizations who have made the game better through their own work; Sabrina Kaley for thumbing through thousands of pages to check the stats; as well as editor Christine Kondo, type-setter Tanya Lloyd Kyi and graphic artist Peter Cocking for their patience, dedication and expertise.

PLAYER AND COACH INDEX

Clarke, Bobby, 72

Cleghorn, Sprague, 66, 126

Cloutier, Dan, 142

Coffey, Paul, 25–26, 49, 60, 114, 116, 169, 170–172, 211

Cole, Danton, 193

Colville, Mac, 113

Colville, Neil, 113

Conacher, Lionel, 44, 138

Conacher, Roy, 212

Connell, Alex, 89, 96, 107, 143

Constantine, Kevin, 111, 140, 141, 155

Cook, Bill, 41, 138, 209

Corbeau, Bert, 93

Corson, Shayne, 198

Cournoyer, Yvan, 193, 206

Coutu, Billy, 65–66

Crawford, Johnny, 82

Crawford, Marc, 101, 149, 165, 200

Crha, Jiri, 92

Crisp, Terry, 155

Crozier, Roger, 148

Cullen, John, 23–24

Cunneyworth, Randy, 118

Dahlen, Ulf, 23

Dahlin, Kjell, 193

Daigneault, Jean-Jacques, 119

Damphousse, Vincent, 7

Dandurand, Leo, 165

Daneyko, Ken, 110, 117–118

Darragh, Jack, 208

Davidson, John, 10, 183

Day, Hap, 26, 217

Dean, Kevin, 193

Delvecchio, Alex, 2, 141, 193

Demers, Jacques, 155

Denneny, Corbett, 209

Denneny, Cy, 66, 93, 117, 209

Denney, Corb, 93

Desjardins, Eric, 212

Dineen, Bill, 193

Dion, Connie, 4

Dion, Michel, 89

Dionne, Marcel, 13, 18–19

Donnelly, Gord, 133

Donnelly, Mike, 110

Doraty, Ken, 17, 187

Dowd, Jim, 193

Drillon, Gordie, 15, 59

Drury, Chris, 174

Dryden, Ken, 85, 88–89, 137, 181–182, 185–186, 193, 213, 216

Dudley, Rick, 10

Duff, Dick, 148

Dupont, Andre, 133

Dupont, Moose, 62

Durnan, Bill, 86, 88, 90, 209

Dutton, Red, 43, 64, 134

Dwyer, Gord, 64

Dye, Babe, 206

Eddolls, Frank, 153

Emberg, Eddie, 177

Esposito, Phil, 1, 10–11, 18–20, 77–79, 97, 130, 153, 155

Esposito, Tony, 90, 95, 196, 215

Evans, Kevin, 62

Eveleigh, Joe, 100

Ezinicki, Bill, 199

Fedorov, Sergei, 17, 49, 69